GNVQ Advanced Options

Financial Services

Anne Harley

First published in 1996 by:
Stanley Thornes (Publishers) Ltd
Ellenborough House
Wellington Street
CHELTENHAM
GL50 1YW
United Kingdom

96 97 98 99 00 / 10 9 8 7 6 5 4 3 2 1

A catalogue record for this book is available from the British Library.

ISBN 0 7487 1913 X

Acknowledgements

The author and publishers are grateful to the following for permission to reproduce photographs:
Digital Stock Corporation (pp, 23, 43); The Body Shop (p. 31); Pictor International (p. 104); Nationwide Building Society (cover photograph)

Typeset by P&R Typesetters Ltd., Salisbury, Wilts
Printed and bound in Great Britain by Scotprint, Musselburgh

Contents

Dedication

With thanks to the B.O.P.S. staff team for all their help and support. For Flash, whose difficulties with this unit helped me to persevere and finish this book.

Introduction

This book is intended for students following the Advanced GNVQ Business course who have chosen Financial Services as an optional unit under either the RSA or BTEC syllabus. It would also be useful to anyone starting their own business or studying any course which involved an element of business planning.

The book is intended to fulfil the needs of students who have to build a portfolio of evidence, but also provides the underpinning and background knowledge required for an understanding of the financial services sector.

How to use this book

The book is divided up into two sections – the descriptive text with activities and assignments, and the Factfile. The activities and assignments are designed to cover all areas of the evidence indicators and will build into a portfolio of evidence suitable for Advanced GNVQ in Business. Many of the assignments provide opportunities for assessment of the NCVQ grading themes as well as contributing evidence for the Core Skills units, Communication, Application of Number and Information Technology.

The Factfile contains additional information about areas covered in the descriptive text. Items that are covered in more detail in the Factfile are to be found in bold type in the text. The Factfile is in alphabetical order to enable students and tutors to access information quickly.

Tutors' note

This book covers the requirements of both the RSA and BTEC syllabus. The main difference between the two is the inclusion of the personal finance section in the RSA syllabus. Tutors following the BTEC version may wish to omit the first chapter, which deals primarily with personal finance. However, experience has shown that students find the otherwise bewildering field of financial services easier when they can relate the information to their own circumstances, and it may well be useful to include some of the first chapter in the course to give students a background which will offer a way in to the subject, and will also give them valuable information and life skills.

Financial services (Advanced)

Element 12.1 Examine the financial services available to businesses

Performance criteria

1 Describe the financial services commonly required by businesses
2 Explain the purposes of the financial services
3 Describe the main providers of the financial services commonly required by business
4 Describe the terms and conditions associated with the provision of financial services commonly required by businesses

Element 12.2 Investigate the financial services required by given businesses

Performance criteria

1 Explain the financial services required by given businesses
2 Describe internal support for financial services requirements in given businesses
3 Describe external support for financial service requirements in given businesses

Element 12.3 Select external providers of financial services to meet the needs of given businesses

Performance criteria

1 Obtain information from external providers for the financial services required by the given businesses
2 Compare the information obtained from external providers
3 Select an external provider for each of the financial services required for each of the given businesses
4 Justify the selection of external providers of the financial services required for the given businesses

Financial services (Advanced)

Element 11.1   Examine financial services providers

Performance criteria

1 Describe the needs for financial services
2 Describe the financial services providers and the financial services they offer
3 Compare financial services offered by financial services providers
4 Describe the recent trends in the development of financial services providers

Element 11.2   Recommend personal financial services for individuals

Performance criteria

1 Describe features of personal financial services offered to individuals by financial services providers
2 Recommend and justify, in terms of client needs, the appropriate personal savings account for different client groups in given situations
3 Recommend and justify, in terms of client needs, the appropriate form of personal credit for different client groups in given situations
4 Recommend and justify, in terms of client needs, the appropriate personal loan for different client groups in given situations

Element 11.3   Recommend financial services for business organisations

Performance criteria

1 Use information sources to identify financial services offered by financial services providers available to business organisations
2 Describe the features of financial services offered by financial services providers
3 Identify and give examples of the financial services that meet the needs of different stages of business development
4 Recommend and justify the appropriate financial services for different stages of business development in given situations

Guide to coverage of the GNVQ Advanced Options

Assignment	11.1	RSA 11.2	11.3	12.1	BTEC 12.2	12.3
Baby's nest egg	●	●				
An account for the boys	●	●				
The career's convention	●	●				
The first car	●	●				
Our first home	●	●				
Buying furniture	●	●				
Retirement	●	●				
Having a gamble	●	●				
Flying away	●	●				
The in-tray	●	●				
Toys for us	●		●	●	●	●
Phil's fast food franchise	●		●	●	●	●
Joe and Susan Lewis	●		●	●	●	●
Jackson Optical Equipment Ltd	●		●	●	●	●
Along the High Street	●			●		
Small Business Advisory Unit	●			●		
G M Cropthorne Ltd	●		●	●	●	●
Marfell Ltd	●		●	●	●	●
Bolton Electrical Services Ltd	●		●	●	●	●
Selecting insurance advice	●		●	●	●	●
Taking stock	●		●	●	●	●
Banking services	●			●		
Going public	●			●		
Hospital concourse				●	●	
Need for financial services in the public sector				●	●	●
Waiving or drowning?	●			●		

I Financial services for individuals

This chapter examines the following:

- How our need for financial services changes as we go through life
- The financial services commonly used by private individuals
- Methods of comparing the services on offer from different providers

Money makes the world go round
  The world go round
    The world go round...

From the cradle to the grave, money is an important part of our lives. While it cannot buy happiness or good health, the absence of money can cause a great deal of stress. It makes sense to make sure that, whether we have a little or a lot, what money we do have is managed and put to work for us whenever possible.

The importance of money can be gauged by the size of the financial services industry and the purpose of this book is to see how the industry provides for the needs of its individual and business customers.

From the moment we are born, money makes an impact on our lives. In the past it has been a tradition to cross a new born baby's palm with silver to ensure prosperity for the future, and still today, many parents and grandparents wish to start planning for the newborn infant's financial future from day one, by putting some money aside for the child as it grows. Most financial organisations realise that this is often very important to parents, and have produced a number of products to fill this major market. Financial institutions have filled this market in a number of different ways, mainly by providing:

- **accounts** that can be opened in the child's name at a **bank** or **building society**
- insurance policies that will provide a sum of money when the child is, say, 18
- lump sum annuities, which are special types of insurance policies that are purchased with a single payment and give a high return over a long period
- National Savings Certificates which are another form of longer term (usually five years) savings, which are sold through the Post Office by the **National Savings Bank**
- insurance policies for certain expenses in the future, for example, school fees.

Most of the High Street organisations provide special facilities for young children, and the promotions which accompany the purchase of such facilities shows how important these are to the organisations concerned.

Choosing an investment that is suitable to meet both the child's and the family's circumstances will depend on a number of factors, for example:

- Is access required to the money at any time?
- Is there a lump sum to be invested?
- Will the family be adding to the investment in the future?
- Would the family wish to invest in monthly instalments?
- How long should the investment be for (5 years, 20 years etc)?

The answers to these questions will provide a clue to the type of investment that would be most suitable.

You will, no doubt, come across a number of different types of organisations that provide alternative types of finance to businesses and individuals. A few years ago, a trip to your local bank manager would have been your only option, but in recent years, the number and range of organisations that provide financial services to business and individuals has expanded beyond recognition. You will come across the following in your research:

- clearing (High Street) banks, such as Lloyds, Barclays, Midland and National Westminster
- finance houses, such as Mercantile Credit, HFC Trust, etc
- building societies, such as the Nationwide, Bradford and Bingley, etc.

Making a choice between providers of financial services will be a topic that we will come across repeatedly during our investigations in this book.

Case study

Baby's nest egg

Fahmina and Andy Rajnat have just given birth to their first baby, and both sets of grandparents have offered to put some money away to provide a 'nest egg' for when the child is older. Other members of the family have also given small amounts of money to the child, and Fahmina and Andy are amazed to find that about £1,000 has been given to them by various members of their families. They obviously wish to invest this sum of money wisely, but would like it to go into a long term investment of some sort so that it is 'out of sight and mind' until the child is 18.

Activity

Investigate the range of investments that would be suitable for Fahmina and Andy's baby. You should approach the following organisations for information:

- a bank
- a building society
- an insurance company
- National Savings (Post Office).

Tip: While you are in the bank or building society, pick up any leaflets that are available to help you in your research later. This may save you another journey.

Assignment
Baby's nest egg

This assignment develops knowledge and understanding of the following elements:

RSA 11.1   Examine financial services providers

RSA 11.2   Recommend personal financial services for individuals

It supports development of the following core skills:

Communication 3.2, 3.4

Your tasks

1 Based on the information given in the case study, 'Baby's Nest Egg', produce a report for Fahmina and Andy which gives details of the information you have gathered in the activity. You should support your report with documented evidence of the range of services you have identified.

2 Give recommendations of two suitable alternative investment possibilities for the £1,000, together with an assessment of the return on the investment at the end of the chosen period of time.

3 You should also indicate any charges that may be made by the provider of the investment and an indication of the risk that may be involved with each investment possibility that you have identified.

As a child grows, most parents realise the advantages of encouraging their offspring to be aware of, and in control of, their own money, and will therefore encourage their child to open an account where they can put their pocket money savings, birthday and Christmas or special occasion money. Most High Street banks and building societies offer such accounts for children from about the age of seven, although accounts for younger children can be opened and operated by the parents. Access to the accounts is often very important. If children are at school they may find it difficult to pay in and withdraw their money outside of school hours. Also, people living in rural areas often have a limited choice of provider for this type of service.

Case study

An account for the boys

Suzy Walker has two young sons, aged seven and nine, and thinks it is time that they began to 'put their pennies' away in a savings account. They live in a small rural town, with limited facilities, so it is important that the account is opened locally. There is a post office in the village, and there is a branch of Lloyd's Bank and offices of the Halifax and Nationwide Building Societies in the next town where they shop twice a week. As the children are at school, they will usually only go shopping with their mum on a Saturday morning, and this is when they would usually want to make use of their account. Suzy is anxious that they should be encouraged to save and is therefore interested in such things as promotions, magazines and similar inducements so that the boys will continue to take an active interest in their savings.

Activity

Research possible savings accounts that would be suitable for the children to open. List the special offers, promotions and 'extras' the various organisations offer to young children.

Assignment
An account for the boys

This assignment develops knowledge and understanding of the following elements:
RSA 11.1   Examine financial services providers
RSA 11.2   Recommend personal financial services for individuals

It supports development of the following core skills:
Communication 3.2, 3.4

Your task

Based on the information given in the case study, 'An account for the boys', write a letter to Suzy giving the outcome from your research, and make recommendations as to which account she should open for her sons.

As an individual grows, their need for financial services also grows. When a young person starts work or goes to university, the need to manage their money effectively becomes very important indeed. The financial organisations realise that if they can sell a bank account or other facilities to a student, or young person starting work, they are likely to stay with that

organisation for a long time. As young graduates have a high future earning potential, it makes sense for the financial institutions to provide special facilities such as interest free overdrafts during their period at college. The range of facilities and promotions offered by the financial organisations is wide, varied and constantly changing, so it can seem bewildering to a young person opening an account for the first time. The range of facilities offered to young people can include:

- current (cheque) accounts
- savings accounts
- ATM (hole in the wall) access cards
- interest free overdrafts
- magazines
- special offers on opening account.

Activity

Investigate the range of current (cheque) accounts and special offers currently available to students.

Assignment
The careers convention

This assignment develops knowledge and understanding of the following elements:
RSA 11.1   Examine financial services providers
RSA 11.2   Recommend personal financial services for individuals

It supports development of the following core skills:
Communication 3.2, 3.3, 3.4

Your task

Your local college is hosting a Careers and Higher Education convention for young people in your area and the students' union has asked you to plan a display entitled 'Your money at Uni'. Using the material collected in the activity, prepare a display for the convention. Your display should give the following information:

- general advice about managing a limited budget
- a comparison of the 'special offers'
- a comparison of the various facilities available from the different organisations including the terms and conditions
- details of any costs involved should the terms of the account be contravened.

Your display should be bright and appealing to the age group for which it is intended, as well as including useful advice appropriate to this group of people.

The use of information processing in this activity could be used as evidence for elements of the Information Technology Skills unit.

One of the first major purchases made by a young person is a car. This apparently simple purchase will require access to a number of different financial services including:

- finance facilities
- insurance.

Getting the money together to buy a car is probably the primary consideration of most young people so we will examine that aspect first.

There are a number of ways to finance a car, depending on (a) whether the car is a new one or second hand, and (b) the purchase price.

There are three main ways of financing in these circumstances:

- a personal loan from a bank or building society
- a **hire purchase** agreement
- a **leasing** agreement.

Methods of finance

Personal loans

Personal loans come in many shapes and sizes, and generally banks and other financial services providers are keen to devise a loan package that suits the needs of the individual. In order to apply for a personal loan, the applicant will be required to fill out a form and provide evidence of their ability to repay the loan. This will usually involve showing evidence of earning by presenting payslips for the previous few months, or if the individual is self-employed, a summary of the business accounts. In the case of a loan for a car, the finance provider may make restrictions as to the age of the car involved.

Hire purchase

A hire purchase agreement is particularly suitable for the purchase of goods such as motor vehicles. These loans are usually arranged through a finance house and allow the individual to spread the cost over a longer period (typically two to five years). A hire purchase agreement differs from a personal loan in that it is tied to the purchase of a particular item, the loan cannot be used for anything else. Also, the asset does not become the property of the purchaser until the final payment has been made. Should the purchaser default on the loan, the asset is returned to the lender (subject to the provisions of the Consumer Credit Act).

Leasing

Under a lease, an individual does not own the asset, but rents or leases it from the owner. Leasing packages have become more commonly available to individuals in recent years, where once they were available to businesses only. A range of leasing packages have been developed, whereby an initial deposit is paid, followed by regular payments, and then at the end of the lease period, there is the option to return the asset to the lessor, or make a lump sum payment to obtain ownership.

The variety of hire purchase and leasing agreements that have developed sometimes makes it difficult to distinguish between the two. Initial payments, repayment periods and the use of large end payments (known as balloon payments) on both schemes can make them appear very similar. However, the two types of finance are treated differently under credit protection laws so it is important to understand the differences between the two schemes.

When comparing the cost of borrowing money, the easiest way is to compare the Annual Percentage Rate (APR) for each option. The APR is a means by which interest rates can be compared over different lengths of time and includes any charges that are made by the lending organisation.

Car insurance

Once the finance has been arranged and the vehicle chosen, it is then necessary to insure it. The law requires that all vehicles used on the road have a minimum of third party liability insurance. This means that the driver of the vehicle is insured against damage that may be done to other vehicles, people including passengers, and other people's property, but it does not insure the owner's vehicle. Should an accident occur, the owner of the vehicle would have to claim compensation from the insurers of the vehicle at fault. As this can be an expensive and lengthy procedure, it is possible to increase the level of insurance from the basic minimum required by law to either third party, fire and theft, which will cover the vehicle if it catches fire or is stolen, or fully comprehensive insurance which is an 'all risks' policy covering the owner's vehicle as well. Insurance can be obtained through a broker, who will deal with a number of **insurance companies**, or directly from an insurance company.

Case study

The first car

Jane is 22 and has recently qualified as an Occupational Therapist. She has managed to save up £2,000 towards a car. She would like to buy something no more than a year old, with an engine size of not more than 1300cc. She has had a look around the showrooms and has identified one or two cars that interest her. She is a bit bewildered by the number of 'special deals' available in the showrooms, and knowing that you are studying Business and Finance, she has asked you for advice.

Activity ————————————————————————————————————

Collect information from one bank, one building society and one car dealership on the different ways of buying a car (i.e. personal loans, hire purchase and leasing.)

Approach one insurance broker and one insurance company for a quotation for motor insurance. The quotation should be for third party only cover and for fully comprehensive.

Assignment
The first car

This assignment develops knowledge and understanding of the following elements:
RSA 11.1   Examine financial services providers
RSA 11.2   Recommend personal financial services for individuals

It supports development of the following core skills:
Communication 3.2, 3.4

Your task

Collate the information you have found in the activity and prepare an oral report to give to your tutor, which advises Jane on the different ways in which she can raise the money to finance her car, and on the different types of insurance available. Your report should compare the costs of borrowing and of insurance, and should contain information about the terms and conditions. Your report should also contain recommendations and conclusions.

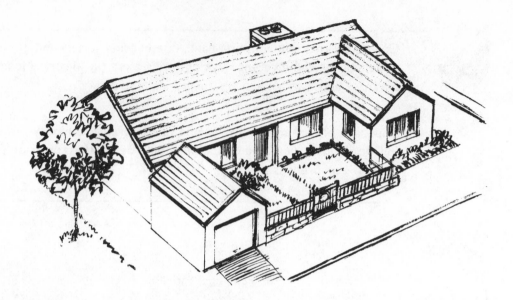

Setting up home is usually the next major step in a person's life, and again, financial services are required to make this possible, whether it is for a mortgage, for house and contents insurance, or for buying furniture, soft furnishings or household equipment.

Setting up home for the first time is a complicated and time-consuming business. It is easy to find that ideas have run away with you and the money runs out before you are finished.

Mortgages

A mortgage is a long-term loan secured by the property. Should the mortgagee not keep up on the repayments, the mortgagor may repossess the property and sell it to repay the debt. There are two main types of mortgage.

Repayment mortgages

This type of loan is repaid in equal monthly instalments, which pays both the interest and repays the capital sum over the period.

Endowment mortgages

This type of loan is linked with a life assurance policy which aims to pay off the capital sum at the end of the loan period. The mortgagor pays interest only on the loan during the period, plus the monthly insurance premium. The assurance policy can be either with or without profits. A policy that is without profits aims just to pay off the capital sum at the end of the period, while a full 'with profits' policy will aim to produce a surplus over and above the capital sum.

Fixed and variable interest mortgages

Mortgages can have either fixed or variable interest rates. A variable interest rate mortgage will reflect changes in the rates of interest in the economy generally, and monthly payments will be altered accordingly. A fixed rate mortgage, however, will remain at the agreed rate for a period of time, often for the first three years or so, but occasionally for the life of the mortgage. Some loans will have a 'catch-up' clause, whereby at the end of the fixed interest period, the lender will calculate the interest that has accrued on a variable rate basis, and adjust the capital sum up or down accordingly.

Case study

Our first home

Claire and John are getting married soon, and have decided to buy their own home. Their joint income (before tax and insurance) is £26,000 per annum, and they have savings of £6,000. They are considering a new starter home which is valued at £40,000.

Activity

Collect information from three possible mortgage lenders and investigate the packages they offer to first time buyers.

Assignment
Our first home

This assignment develops knowledge and understanding of the following elements:

RSA 11.1   Examine financial services providers
RSA 11.2   Recommend personal financial services for individuals

It supports development of the following core skills:
Communication 3.2, 3.4

Your task

From the information you have gathered, prepare a guide for first time buyers. The guide should cover the different types of mortgages available and the advantages and disadvantages of each type.

Insurance

There are a number of different types of insurance that Claire and John would have to consider when purchasing their first home: mortgage protection insurance; building insurance; and home contents insurance.

Mortgage protection insurance

This type of insurance is intended to protect both the borrower and the lender should the borrower become unable to work due to sickness or redundancy. In the past this has often been thought of as an 'added extra', but with changes to the way in which income support and housing benefits are to be paid, it may soon be essential, and maybe even become a condition of the loan that such a policy is taken out. This would ensure that the repayments on the mortgage are paid should one of the insured events (i.e. sickness or redundancy) happen to the borrowers.

Buildings insurance

This type of policy insures the property against damage by such things as fire, subsidence and accidental damage, and will often include a third party liability in case something happens to the property which causes death or injury to a third party; a slate coming off the roof, perhaps, and injuring a passer-by or damaging someone else's property. Most lenders require that such a policy is taken out.

Home contents insurance

A policy of this sort insures the contents of a property, that is the furniture and fittings, against loss or damage through fire, theft, flooding or various other insured events. The owner of the property can choose the level of cover that they require, from basic replacement value to all risks cover on a 'new for old' basis. Individual high value items such as jewellery and art work can be included on the policy. The level of cover is usually determined by how much the policyholder wishes to pay. This type of policy will sometimes cover items in the garden or garage surrounding the property, such as lawnmowers, tools and occasionally even plants and garden ornaments. Home contents insurance is very useful, but not an essential for a young couple setting up home for the first time, especially if they are on a limited budget and the contents of their home are not of any great value.

Many lenders offer insurance facilities to home buyers, and it is often convenient to arrange insurance cover at the same time as arranging a mortgage. The packages arranged by the lenders, however, may not always be the best value for money, and it makes sense to shop around. It is illegal for a lender to insist that a borrower arranges the insurance through them, but may make it a condition of a special offer, such as a low rate fixed interest loan.

Additional advice and assistance

The legal side of buying a house is called 'conveyancing' and, while it is possible to do this yourself, most people engage the services of a solicitor or specialist conveyancing firm. Solicitors and specialist conveyancing firms can be found in most towns, and will be listed in Yellow Pages or the local business directory. Most people will select a solicitor on the personal recommendation of friends or families, or by their reputation in their town.

Activity

Contact a solicitor and a specialist conveyancing firm and find out the costs that Claire and John would be likely to incur in the purchase of their starter home. Ask for a brief description of the process involved and how the costs are incurred.

Once they have bought their new home, Claire and John would have to think about how to find the money to furnish it. The main ways would be by:

- cash
- a personal loan
- hire purchase
- store credit account card
- credit card.

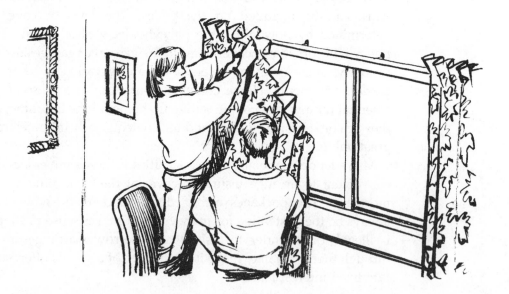

Personal loans and hire purchase will be much the same as we found for financing a car. Store account cards and credit cards are the additional source of funds for this type of purchase, each having their advantages and disadvantages.

Credit cards

The most commonly issued credit cards are Visa and Access. Both cards are accepted in a wide range of outlets for the purchase of just about any type of goods and services. The account holder will be issued with a credit limit, and an account is sent each month. The card holder then has the option to pay any amount between a stated minimum and the full amount due each month. If the full amount is paid by the due date, no interest is charged, giving the cardholder somewhere in the region of up to six weeks free credit. If the full amount is not paid, then interest is charged on the balance and added to the account. Cash can also be withdrawn from an automated teller machine for which a standard charge is made. Purchases made with a credit card entitle the card holder to special consumer protection with regard to theft, faulty goods or goods purchased on mail order that do not arrive.

Advantages — credit cards can provide a flexible way to finance purchases, particularly if the card holder is paid monthly. Credit cards are accepted worldwide, and money in local currency can be obtained from cash machines in most countries. The extra consumer protection is also an added benefit.

Disadvantages — credit cards can be an expensive way of borrowing. If credit is required for more than a month or two, then it may be cheaper to investigate other ways of financing the purchase, for example, a personal loan. As credit cards are so widely accepted, it is easy to over-spend and to stretch the budget beyond what was intended.

Store account cards

There are two main types of store accounts. One, often called an option account, functions in a similar way to a credit card in that the amount paid each month can be varied. The minimum amount is usually deducted from the cardholder's bank account by direct debit, leaving the cardholder with the option to pay the full amount by other means if they so wish.

The other type of account, called different things by different companies, involves a fixed sum standing order or direct debit, payable monthly.

Advantages — store account customers are often entitled to special offers, special shopping evenings and events run by the company.

Disadvantages — store credit cards can be a very expensive way of financing goods. The cards are only valid at certain branches or associated stores and generally do not have a cash facility. They are not usually accepted abroad.

Case study

Buying furniture

Having purchased their new starter home, John and Claire are getting ready to furnish it. After paying the deposit for the house and all of the expenses, they have about £1,000 left from their savings. They realise that they will not be able to afford to buy everything new for their home, and expect that they can pick up some second hand furniture fairly cheaply. They have decided to buy some things new, such as carpets, curtains and a new bed.

Their monthly income and expenditure looks as follows:

	£	£
Joint income (nett)		1,500
Mortgage	300	
Insurance	50	
Gas and electric	80	
Telephone	25	
Food	200	
Car expenses	80	
Socialising	100	
Savings	50	885
Monthly surplus		615

They have calculated that furnishing their home with the basic essentials will cost £2,500. Claire has been looking in the local department store and has found most of the items that they require there. They have offered her a store card to finance her purchases, but John thinks that it looks a bit expensive. They are also wary of over-extending their finances, for, although they are currently reasonably well off, they are aware how fast that could change should either of them become ill or lose their job.

Activity

Investigate the comparative costs of a store card, a credit card and a personal loan for the items they wish to purchase.

Assignment
Buying furniture

This assignment develops knowledge and understanding of the following elements:

RSA 11.1   Examine financial services providers

RSA 11.2   Recommend personal financial services for individuals

It supports development of the following core skills:

Communication 3.2, 3.4

Your task

Based on the information given in the case study, 'Buying Furniture', write a report for Claire and John based on your findings from the activity. Your report should include details of the providers of the facilities you have investigated, and give conclusions and recommendations on which they can base a decision about how to finance their purchases.

The need for financial services continues throughout life, with services available to help people manage their money no matter what their circumstances are. As people get older, their need for financial services changes, with the emphasis being more on investments and planning for retirement than the need for credit to finance purchases for the house and home.

Many people are lucky enough to acquire a large lump sum later in life, either from an occupational pension scheme, redundancy payments, an inheritance, or just good fortune. However, in this day and age, even a large sum of money can disappear rapidly if it is not invested wisely. For people who are getting older, it is often more important to find a safe investment for their money than to maximise their return, which often also means increased risk. There are a range of investment opportunities available, some totally safe, and some with a degree of risk. The safest investments are those with a guaranteed return, such as fixed interest or index-linked investments. Index-linking ties the return on the investment with the Retail Price Index, guaranteeing that inflation will not erode the investment during the savings period.

As a general rule, the higher the risk, the higher the potential return. Probably the most uncertain investment is a venture capital fund or investment in the stock market. The potential returns can be very high, but there is a risk of losing the investment altogether, a risk that most people would not like to take.

Of the investment opportunities commonly available, the following types of investment are the most usual.

High interest savings

Available at most banks and building societies, this type of account offers a higher rate of interest providing 90 days' notice of withdrawal is given. There is a minimum amount (usually £1,000 but sometimes more) that is needed to open the account.

TESSAs

A Tax Exempt Special Savings Account (TESSA) can be opened with most banks and building societies. A lump sum or up to thirteen payments per year can be invested in the account which lasts for five years. The interest is tax free and can either be added to the account or taken out each year. There is a maximum amount that can be invested each year during the life of the account. Rates of return vary from provider to provider, but are generally around 2-3 per cent above normal investment rates, and there is often a bonus payable at the end of the period.

PEPs

Personal Equity Plans (PEPs) enable an individual to invest in a portfolio of shares which are then put into a special fund where they must remain for a minimum of five years. The proceeds are free of both income and capital gains tax.

National Savings Certificates

The National Savings Bank offers a range of savings plans often known as 'Granny Bonds', but in recent years, the opportunities available have broadened. The savings plans are either index-linked or fixed interest plans, where a lump sum is invested for a period of five years, free of income tax.

Savings linked endowment policies

Longer term investments are usually provided by some form of savings linked insurance policy. These can be bought either with a lump sum, or by regular monthly payments. The length of the investment can be anything from 10 to 30 years. The longer the term, the greater the return. These policies do not give a guaranteed return, as the bonuses are dependent on the company profits, but they have proved to be useful investments during the past 20 years giving better returns than most alternatives. They also have the added advantage of providing additional life assurance cover.

Case study

Retirement

Winston and Sylvia have recently retired. Winston, from his job in the civil service, and Sylvia from her job as a nurse. Both have an occupational pension, part of which they have commuted to receive lump sum payments. After paying off what remained owing on their mortgage, they have both the time and the resources to indulge themselves. Winston's family originated in Jamaica, and he has had a long-term ambition to return to the Caribbean for an extended holiday and to visit friends and relatives. As they are both relatively young (58 and 55) they realise that their money will have to provide them with an income for quite some time to come, and so they want to make sure that it is invested wisely before they take off on their long-awaited trip abroad. As they are intending to be away from home for about three months, they want to make sure that their financial situation is settled before they leave.

Activity

Winston and Sylvia have decided to put £10,000 into a long-term investment that will provide a monthly income. Safety is as important as return on their investment, as they cannot afford to lose money. Investigate the investment possibilities for them.

Assignment
Retirement

This assignment develops knowledge and understanding of the following elements:

RSA 11.1   Examine financial services providers

RSA 11.2   Recommend personal financial services for individuals

It supports development of the following core skills:

Communication 3.2, 3.4

Your task

Summarise your findings from the activity in the form of a report, with conclusions and recommendations.

Case study

Having a gamble

Winston has always fancied a gamble on the stock market, and they have decided that they can afford £2,000. They realise that, while there is a chance of making a very high return on their money, equally, there is the chance of losing it all, particularly as Winston has no real experience in dealing with stocks and shares.

Activity

Contact a bank, a building society and a broker and find out what facilities they offer in terms of help and advice. You should also investigate the costs involved in buying shares on the stock market.

Assignment
Having a gamble

This assignment develops knowledge and understanding of the following elements:
RSA 11.1   Examine financial services providers
RSA 11.2   Recommend personal financial services for individuals

It supports development of the following core skills:
Communication 3.2, 3.4

Your task

From the information you have gathered, produce a pamphlet entitled 'A beginner's guide to stocks and shares'.

Case study

Flying away

Having sorted out their domestic finances, Winston and Sylvia are ready to take their holiday to Jamaica. They are concerned that while they are away, there will still be bills to be paid, and are not sure how to achieve this by 'remote control'. They are also uncertain of the best way to ensure that they have enough money on their trip.

Activity

Approach the four main High Street banks (Midland, Lloyds, National Westminster and Barclays) and find out what facilities they can offer to Winston and Sylvia.

Assignment
Flying away

This assignment develops knowledge and understanding of the following elements:
RSA 11.1   Examine financial services providers
RSA 11.2   Recommend personal financial services for individuals

It supports development of the following core skills:
Communication 3.2, 3.4

Your task

Compile a report for Winston and Sylvia which summarises your findings and provides them with the information they need to make a decision on how to make sure their bills are paid, and how to make enough money available to them while they are away.

Review your progress

1 List the different types of investments that are available for investing a lump sum for a small child.

2 What criteria can be used to select a savings account for a child?

3 How do banks and building societies differ in the services they provide for their personal customers?

4 List the range of services offered by the High Street banks to young people going to university.

5 What is the difference between a hire purchase agreement and a lease?

6 Which organisations are most frequently the providers of lease and hire purchase agreements?

7 What is APR, and how can it be used?

8 What is a mortgage?

9 What are the main types of mortgages currently available for personal customers?

10 What is the difference between a fixed rate and a variable rate mortgage?

11 What is mortgage protection insurance?

12 What are the main types of insurance normally taken out by property owners?

13 What is conveyancing?

14 How do credit cards work?

15 What are the advantages and disadvantages of store account cards?

16 What are TESSAs and PEPs?

Assignment
The in-tray

This assignment develops knowledge and understanding of the following elements:
RSA 11.1   Examine financial services providers
RSA 11.2   Recommend personal financial services for individuals

It supports development of the following core skills:
Communication 3.2, 3.4

You are on work experience with one of the High Street banks and, as part of your training, you have been asked to draft letters in reply to the following letters suggesting which of the bank's facilities would be of use in solving the problems outlined. You should include with your replies suitable brochures which would give the clients additional information.

21 High Street
Newtown
Anyshire

Dear Sir

I shall be going to university in a couple of months time, and
would be grateful for some advice. I have never had a bank
account before, but my Dad has banked with you for years and says
that I can't go far wrong with you.

    Could you please tell me what sort of account I need, and how I
go about opening it.

Many thanks,

Joan Tyler

Joan Tyler (Miss)

Little Oaks
Oakway Farm
Uphampton
Anyshire

Dear Sirs

*My wife and I have recently moved into the above address with our
three children, and we are thinking of replacing the carpets and
soft furnishings. There are also a number of jobs that need doing
around the place, such as re-plastering the back room walls, and
replacing the bathroom window frame.*

    *We are unsure of the best way to raise the money. I suppose we
will need about £2,500 in all.*

    *We are thinking of having the carpets and things on HP, but the
offer in the shop looks a bit expensive.*

    *I would be most grateful if you could advise us on what you
could offer. We have banked with you for about 10 years now.*

Yours faithfully

J. M. Eaton

3 The Almshouses
Highfield Lane
Newtown
Anyshire

Dear Sirs

I would be most grateful if you could give me some advice. When my husband died last year, the insurance people sent me quite a large sum of money which has been sitting in my current account ever since. My son says that I really should be getting more interest on it, but I am not quite sure what I should do. You see, my pension isn't really enough to cover my bills and everything, so I will probably need to draw on it from time to time. On the other hand, I can't afford to pass up the chance of extra interest.

Could you please let me know what sort of savings account I could put this money into, that would give me a good rate of interest, but also let me have access to my money should there be a disaster of some sort?

Yours faithfully

K Perrett

Kate Perrett (Mrs)

2 Starting up in business

This chapter examines the following:

- Methods of going into business for the first time
- The need for financial services in the early stages of a business

The life cycle of businesses

In the first chapter of this book, we looked at how an individual's need for financial services will change as they develop and grow. In a similar way, a business will pass through a number of stages from the time that the owner(s) of the business have the original idea, until the business is eventually wound up, taken over, or the original owners decide to sell. These stages can be likened to the human life cycle: birth, adolescence and maturity.

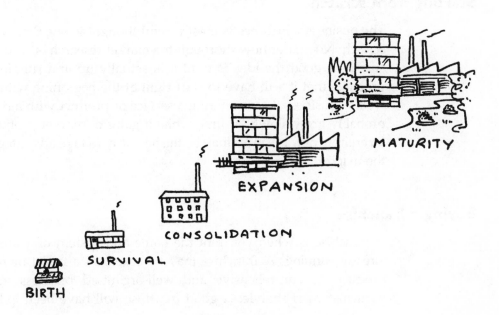

MATURITY

EXPANSION

CONSOLIDATION

SURVIVAL

BIRTH

Unlike its human counterpart, however, a business is constantly changing its shape, organisational structure and sometimes its ownership, to respond to changes in the outside world — such as the economic climate, changes in its markets — and in order to achieve its organisational objectives, which for most trading organisations, is maximisation of profits. In the remaining chapters of the book, we will be investigating how business needs change as the business passes through the various stages of growth; the financial services that it will require as it develops; and the organisations that will provide the services to meet those needs.

Ways of going into business

There are many ways of going into business for the first time: you can start from scratch with a new idea or product; you can buy into an existing business, by buying a **franchise** or a **partnership** for example; or you can buy a '**going concern**', maybe from someone who had decided to retire. No matter which route is decided upon, you are going to need money, advice and support, and there are a wide variety of organisations ready and willing to sell you what you need. Some of the needs of a new business will be the same, no matter which route is preferred, but some needs will be specific to a particular type of organisation, or will be best met by a particular source.

Starting from scratch

The business which needs most careful thought is one that is started from scratch. No matter how thorough the market research is, you can never be sure how good the idea is until it is actually up and running. It is quite probable that it will have to start right at the beginning with premises as well. A business that is offering a service or product with a difference will probably grow slowly at first, while it gains a 'market profile'. However, an entirely new business may be the best way to take advantage of a gap in the market.

Buying a franchise

A franchise is when you rent the name and system of a business that is already running. A franchise may be based on a novel or revolutionary product, a comprehensive and well-organised business method, or a particular market style. A good franchise will have been 'piloted' by the

franchiser for a number of years so that all the potential problems have been sorted out, and it has been proved that the business idea can be successfully repeated. Buying a franchise can take a great deal of the risk out of starting in business for the first time, and the chances of failure in the first three years are reduced. The price of choosing the franchise route into a new business can, however, be high but the number of High Street franchises in existence (The Body Shop and McDonald's to name but two) proves the success of the franchising system.

Buying into a partnership

For many professional people, buying into a partnership is the usual way of establishing their business. For many newly qualified doctors, dentists, vets, accountants and solicitors, buying into an existing partnership is the normal way of starting their professional practice. Many of the difficulties that arise from starting a new venture can be avoided in this way, as the new starter has a group of experienced partners to show him the ropes in the early years. It is important, however, to ensure the financial stability of any partnership that is bought, as each partner is 'severally and jointly liable' for any debts of the business. That means that any of the partners may be sued for the whole amount of the business's debts!

Buying a going concern

Whether it is a large organisation, or the local corner shop, buying a going concern, perhaps from an owner who is retiring or by obtaining a controlling interest in a limited company, can have its advantages. The business will already have premises, stock and a market profile, together with financial statements that can show how successful the business has been in the past. The price you pay for a business, however, will be more than the value placed on the **assets**. This surplus is called **goodwill**, which will represent the reputation of the business, and its existing customers. The valuation of goodwill can be a haphazard operation, and there is no guarantee that existing customers will stay with the new owner of the business, or that existing suppliers will agree to trade with the new owner on the same terms and conditions as before, and the value of goodwill could quickly vanish under the new management.

Management buy-outs

Management buy-outs have become a feature of the 1980s and 1990s, where part of a business becomes a separate company, owned and managed by the former managers. Many large companies have sold parts of their business to former managers, for a variety of reasons:

- the part of the business sold may be on the periphery of the main business of the company
- it may be a loss-making part of the company that local management feel able to turn into profit.

IBM, British Coal, the former British Rail, ICI and Dowty's are just a few of the household names that have sold parts of their business to former managers during the last 15 or so years.

Activity

1 What criteria would you use for choosing a method of going into business?
2 What would be the advantages and disadvantages of forming a partnership to set up a new business?
3 What things would the two partners in a new venture have to agree upon before starting out, to avoid problems in the future?

Whichever method is chosen, and this will depend on the type of business being set up, the amount of money available etc, one of the first things that needs to be done is to produce a **business plan**.

The business plan

In order to decide on the amount of money that will be needed in the early months of a new business, it will be necessary to devise a business plan. This will provide a blueprint of the business and will include such information as the objectives of the business, the market, details of the product or service, and information on premises, equipment, personnel and marketing and promotion. One of the main ingredients of a business plan, is the **cash flow forecast**, which contains the information that any prospective lender will want to study in detail before deciding the amount, and the terms and conditions, of any loan they may provide. In basic terms, the cash flow forecast will detail the expected incomings and outgoings of the business during the first six months to a year of trading, and will identify any shortfall that may occur during that time. From the cash flow forecast, the prospective lender can see both the amount of finance that will be needed during the initial period, and can also estimate the element of risk involved in lending to this new business.

Let us have a look at a typical cash flow forecast from the business plan of a new venture, and see if we can identify the various financial needs that the business will have during the first year of trading.

Case study

Toys for us

Phillipa Jones has inherited £6,000 from an aunt, and has decided to set up her own business. For many years, Phillipa has been interested in making wooden toys, which she has done as a hobby using her garage as a workshop. She would now like to develop her hobby into a full-time business, by renting a workshop at the local Heritage Centre, which would have the advantage of being able to sell her goods to the tourists who come and visit the centre. She also hopes to sell her toys at craft fairs and exhibitions during the winter months when the visitors to the Heritage Centre are few. She has produced a cash flow forecast to help her identify any additional finance she will need during her first six months of trading. Phillipa has estimated that it will take two years for her reputation to be fully established, when she anticipates that her sales will reach an average of £2,000 per month. She feels she will need new equipment and a van to add to the equipment that she has already accumulated to make her business viable.

	January	February	March	April	May
Income					
Sales	400	500	600	700	800
Total income	400	500	600	700	800
Expenditure					
Van	2900				
Equipment	1800				
Rent	100	100	100	100	100
Heat and light			250		
Materials		400	200	300	350
Van expenses	100	100	100	100	100
Drawings	400	400	400	400	400
Total expenditure	5300	1000	1050	900	950
Surplus/deficit for month	(-4900)	(-500)	(-450)	(-200)	(-150)
Capital	6000				
Balance b/f	0	1100	600	150	(-50)
Balance c/f	1100	600	150	(-50)	(-200)

In the forecast that she has produced, Phillipa has decided to finance these needs from her own **capital**, but that may not be the best way for her to proceed.

You can see straight away from the case study that Phillipa will have a monthly deficit quite quickly, and a cash flow deficit by April, but in order to decide the best way in which to deal with this, it is necessary to look more closely at her financial needs, and classify them in some way. The most convenient way is to divide those needs into long-term needs, i.e. money that is needed for more than a year, and short-term needs, money that is required for a year or less. It is also useful to decide if the finance is needed for working capital — that is money needed to ensure she has enough to pay her debts, or to buy assets.

Activity

From the cash flow forecast that Phillipa has prepared, identify the following financial needs of her new business:

- long-term finance — finance required for more than one year
- short-term finance — finance required for less than one year
- finance of working capital — to ensure the business has enough cash to pay its debts
- finance for the purchase of assets — such as vehicles, machinery, etc.

In groups of four or five, brainstorm alternative ways in which Phillipa might find the money to finance her new business.

Remember — to brainstorm effectively, you should list all the ideas you have, even if some of them seem a bit unlikely at first. But now, you must evaluate the ideas that you have come up with.

Assignment
Toys for us

This assignment develops knowledge and understanding of the following elements:

RSA 11.1   Examine financial services providers
RSA 11.3   Recommend financial services for business organisations
BTEC 12.1   Examine the financial services available to businesses
BTEC 12.2   Investigate the financial services required by given businesses
BTEC 12.3   Select external providers of financial services to meet the needs of given businesses

It supports development of the following core skills:
Communication 3.2, 3.4

Your tasks

From your brainstorming list, select one source of finance each and investigate the following:

- Find at least two different types of organisation that could provide that type of finance.

35

- List the costs involved with borrowing from each organisation.
- Compile a list of advantages and disadvantages of meeting the financial needs of the new business in this way.

Sorting out the financial needs of a new venture is obviously very important. The number of business failures each year is closely related to inadequate finance (and often over-optimistic forecasting) particularly the finance of working capital, but the need for money is only one of many needs a new business has.

Needs other than money

Help and advice is often required on a wide range of organisational issues when someone is starting in business for the first time. You need to be able to calculate how much profit you are making, for example, and to ensure you know how much you own, and how much you owe. You need to make sure you know who owes you money, and for how long, and find ways of making sure you get paid. Advice on such things as pensions, insurance and taxation can also ensure that the business does not run into trouble at a later date. Let us have a look at some of these issues in detail.

Activity

1 Make a list of all the things that you might need additional help and advice with if you were going into business for the first time.
2 Who do you think you might approach for this type of assistance?
3 How would you go about finding the help and advice you might need?

Record keeping

The ultimate survival of a business will be helped by its financial record keeping, which will ensure that it will know how much cash it needs to pay its creditors when they are due, and will also be able to ensure that they are trading at a profit, i.e. selling their goods and services for more than they cost to produce. Good financial records are also very helpful when dealing with the Tax Inspector. Accounts have to be prepared at the end of each financial year and sent to the Tax Inspector, and if the business is a limited company, profit and loss statements and a **balance sheet** have to be prepared at the end of each accounting year.

Good record keeping will also aid in the good management of the business by:

- allowing management to know the current positions of the business
- providing information which can aid decision making
- providing evidence that can be used when raising additional finance in the future.

There are also a number of statutory (legal) requirements that some businesses must comply with, contained in the Companies Acts and the partnership agreements. In addition, records will aid in the accurate assessment of:

- **VAT** (value added tax)
- income tax
- National Insurance contributions.

It makes a great deal of sense for a new business to select and maintain a suitable system of record keeping right from the beginning, to avoid any difficulties arising at a later date.

Activity

1 Why do you think it is important for a business to have a good system of financial record keeping?
2 How do you think the needs of the business might differ if they were:
   a a small shopkeeper
   b a medium sized manufacturing business
   c a PLC.

Types of record-keeping systems

While all record-keeping systems follow the same accounting procedures, the way that the theory is translated into practice can vary quite considerably. There would be no need, for example, for a small business such as Phillipa Jones's, to keep a full double entry system of accounting. She could probably manage very well on an analysed cash book system, which would provide all the information she would need in a very simple form. On the other hand, a larger and more complex organisation would find it very difficult if it relied only on an analysed cash book to meet their management needs.

Selecting a record-keeping system

In order to select a suitable record-keeping system, it is necessary for an organisation to take the following into consideration.

Time and skills available

- Will the owner be responsible for completing the records?
- How much knowledge does the owner of the business have about book-keeping?
- Will a book-keeper be employed?
- Will an accountant be used?

Activity

I What sort of time and skills do you think would be available to small sole traders to look after their book-keeping requirements?

2 How do you think that they could overcome any limitations that they might have?

Computerised or manual accounts

- Will the business have a computer system that can take a computerised accounting package?
- What would be the cost of setting up a computer system solely for accounting purposes?

Management information

- How much information will the management of the business require to effectively control the operations of the business?
- Will the business be legally required to submit or publish accounts?
- What responsibilities does the business have to produce financial information to outsiders (e.g. the **bank**)?

Activity

I Compare the demands that may be made on an accounting system by:
a a partnership
b a private limited company
c a public limited company.

Future requirements

- Are the business needs likely to change with the next few years?
- Will the business be looking for additional finance in the next three years, when information will be required to support any additional loans?

When all these questions have been answered, the business will be in a strong position to select a suitable system of recording financial information that will meet the needs of the business, both in the short and in the long term.

Case study

> **Phil's fast food franchise**
>
> Phil has decided to buy a franchise from a national fast food operation. He has managed to raise the finance from a number of sources, including his local High Street bank. He is deciding what form his financial record keeping should take.
>
> In addition to keeping track of his day-to-day transactions, he has identified the following business needs that the system should be able to cope with:
>
> 1 returns to the franchiser
> 2 returns to Customs and Excise for VAT
> 3 returns to the Inland Revenue for tax purposes
> 4 final accounts.
>
> The business already has an up-to-date computer which is used for word-processing, and Phil has some book-keeping experience. He intends to use an accountant to produce the final accounts, but he wants to keep the costs down by providing him with as complete a set of records at the end of year as he can.

Activity

Using the information in the case study, investigate two possible computer software packages that might be useful to Phil.

Assignment
Phil's fast food franchise

This assignment develops knowledge and understanding of the following elements:

RSA 11.1   Examine financial services providers

RSA 11.3   Recommend financial services for business organisations

BTEC 12.1   Examine the financial services available to businesses

BTEC 12.2   Investigate the financial services required by given businesses

BTEC 12.3   Select external providers of financial services to meet the needs of given businesses

It supports development of the following core skills:
Communication 3.2, 3.4

Your task

From the information gathered in the activity, write a short report detailing:

- the cost of the packages
- an evaluation of their suitability
- advantages and disadvantages of each package
- recommendations as to which package to buy.

Insurance

Anyone who is in business needs insurance. Without it the livelihood of the owner and the employees is at risk. In addition, there are some types of insurance that are compulsory by law. In today's insurance market, almost any risk can be insured against — at a price — but let us look at the types of insurance that are required by law, together with the most common types of insurance that a business might need.

Legal liabilities

Running a business creates considerable legal responsibilities towards employees, the public and customers. Liability insurance will indemnify the business for awards made against it by the courts in the form of damages, claimant's costs and expenses.

Employers' liability

By law, all employers must insure against their legal liabilities for injury, disease or death to employees sustained by them and arising from their employment. Employees will normally include apprentices and other trainees, and those hired from another employer. Businesses are legally required to insure for at least £2 million, but in practice, most policies offer unlimited liability. The law also requires that a certificate of employers' liability is displayed at each place of work.

Public liability

Public liability insurance covers the legal liability to pay damages to members of the public for death, bodily injury or damage to their property which occurs as a result of business activities. It also covers legal fees, costs and expenses such as representation at any coroner's inquest, fatal accident enquiry or other court hearing because of an accident.

Motor vehicle liability

Businesses are required to insure their vehicles in the same way as private individuals, for injury to others and damage to their property arising from the use of vehicles on the road.

Activity

1 Why do you think that the law has intervened to make it compulsory for a business to take out certain types of insurance?
2 If you were in charge of the whole country, what other events would you make it compulsory for business to take out insurance against?

Property

Buildings and their contents can be insured against **fire**, lightning and explosion of gas and boilers. 'Special perils' such as explosion, riot, malicious damage, storm, flood, impact by aircraft, road and rail vehicles, escape of water from tanks or pipes and sprinkler leakage can also be included.

Engineering

Engineering insurance provides cover against electrical or mechanical breakdown for most machinery, including computers. By law, many items of plant such as boilers, lifts and lifting machinery must be inspected regularly by a qualified person. Insurers can arrange to provide this service.

Theft

Contents can be covered against **theft**, providing there has been forcible and violent entry to, or exit from, the premises. Damage to the building resulting from theft or attempted theft can also be covered.

Theft by employees

Theft of money or stock arising from dishonesty of employees is usually covered by a policy known as a Fidelity Guarantee.

Goods in transit

Goods in transit insurance covers goods against loss or damage while in a vehicle owned by the business, or when sent by carrier.

Business interruption

Business interruption insurance can compensate a business for the short-fall in gross profits together with paying any increased working costs and extra accountant fees should business property be damaged.

Health insurance

People who are self-employed are not able to claim sickness benefit if they are unable to work. There are two types of policy available which pay a regular income to compensate for the loss of earnings through accident, sickness or incapacity. They are personal accident and sickness insurance, which makes regular payments on a weekly basis for a maximum number of weeks, and permanent **health insurance**, which pays a regular income while the insured is unable to work, up to the end of the policy term.

Case study

Joe and Susan Lewis

Joe and Susan Lewis have recently bought a grocery shop and are concerned about what sort of insurance they might need.

Assignment
Joe and Susan Lewis

This assignment develops knowledge and understanding of the following elements:

RSA 11.1   Examine financial services providers

RSA 11.3   Recommend financial services for business organisations

BTEC 12.1   Examine the financial services available to businesses

BTEC 12.2   Investigate the financial services required by given businesses

BTEC 12.3   Select external providers of financial services to meet the needs of given businesses

It supports development of the following core skills:
Communication 3.2, 3.4.

Produce a short report for Sue and Joe, which explains the different types of insurance and makes recommendations as to which types might be worth considering for a business such as theirs.

Pensions

A self-employed person is required to pay Class 2 National Insurance contributions which will entitle them to a state pension on retirement. However, most self-employed people will want to make arrangement for the time when they retire by taking out a private pension plan, organised and invested by an insurance company. Payments into such a plan qualify for tax relief and the money is put into a tax-free fund. Personal pension plans are usually very flexible, allowing the investor to start receiving payments at any time between their fiftieth and seventy-fifth birthday. There is also usually a facility which makes an allowance for early retirement due to ill health.

There are many schemes currently on the market, but they generally fall into three main categories.

Non-profit

These pension plans are for a guaranteed pension at the end of the term. They provide a fixed sum, specified at the time the plan is taken out, and while they are of limited value, they are fully guaranteed.

With profits

The insurance company will guarantee a minimum pension or lump sum at the end of the term. While the guaranteed sum will be less than the non-profit policy, the investor can receive a much higher pension as the insurance company will add bonuses to the pension depending on the profits made on its investments.

Unit linked

The value of the pension in a unit-linked plan is directly linked to the value of a choice of investments. Commonly, the investor can choose for the money to be invested in property, shares, fixed interest investments such as British Government stocks, cash investments or a mixture of these. The main problem with unit linked policies is the fact that the value of these investments can fluctuate, and values could be low at the time of retirement.

Activity

Research has shown that large numbers of people who do not have a company pension scheme (that is both employed and self-employed people) have not taken out a large enough pension scheme to provide them with a sufficient income when they retire.

Discuss the reasons why people are reluctant to take out an adequate pension plan.

Case study

Jackson Optical Equipment Ltd

Jackson Optical Equipment Ltd is a new private limited company being set up by two brothers, Mike and Bill Jackson. Bill is a engineer who has recently been made redundant and Mike has just completed a degree in Business and Finance at Birmingham University. The company will manufacture specialised optical equipment for the construction industry, in a small factory outside Dudley.

Mike and Bill are concerned that they could be sued if one of their pieces of equipment should fail and cause injury or damage to property.

Activity

They have asked you to investigate the possibility of taking out product liability insurance to protect them should this occur.

Assignment
Jackson Optical Equipment Ltd

This assignment develops knowledge and understanding of the following elements:

RSA 11.1   Examine financial services providers
RSA 11.3   Recommend financial services for business organisations
BTEC 12.1   Examine the financial services available to businesses
BTEC 12.2   Investigate the financial services required by given businesses
BTEC 12.3   Select external providers of financial services to meet the needs of given businesses

It supports development of the following core skills:
Communication 3.2, 3.4.

Your task

Based on the information given in the case study, produce a short report for Mike and Bill which compares two sources of product liability insurance. Your report should contain information on the following:

- possible sources
- costs
- cover
- advantages and disadvantages of each policy.

Sources of help and advice

In addition to professional advisors, there are a large number of organisations designed to help new or small businesses. Many are self-help organisations, or organisations set up on a non-profit making basis to give support to local businesses.

Training and Enterprise Councils

Training and Enterprice Councils (TECs) provide advice and counselling to businesses in their area. The services provided will vary and are decided upon by individual TECs to meet local needs.

47

Activity

1 Contact your local TEC and find out what services they provide for businesses in your area.
2 Draft a booklet entitled 'A guide to your TEC' aimed at people going into business for the first time, which will give them an insight into what services are provided.

Local enterprise agencies

Local enterprise agencies are non-profit making organisations set up to help and advise small businesses. There are more than 300 such organisations throughout the UK, but each one is different in the way it is funded and the services they offer. Normally, however, their services will include free and confidential business information and advice, training courses, advice on property and the provision of workshop units, and advice on the availability of grants and loans.

Department of Trade and Industry Enterprise Initiative

Under the DTI's enterprise initiative, small businesses can get consultancy on a number of topics including marketing, design, quality, manufacturing systems, business planning, financial and information systems and exports. The business will pay between half and two thirds of the cost of the consultancy.

Local Chambers of Trade and Commerce

Local Chambers of Trade and Commerce can provide a wide range of information and advice to local business people, tailored to local requirements. They often provide monthly or quarterly bulletins to keep people up to date. Services provided will vary from district to district.

Review your progress

1 What are the advantages and disadvantages of starting a new business from scratch?
2 What is a franchise? Can you name any famous High Street businesses that are franchise organisations?

3 What is a manangement buy-out?

4 Why is it important to produce a business plan before going into business for the first time?

5 What sort of information will be included in a business plan?

6 What are the main requirements of a good financial record-keeping system? Why is it important to the business?

7 Which forms of insurance must a business have by law?

8 What is business interruption insurance, and what sort of business would need to have it?

9 What is the diference between a non-profit and a with-profits pension?

10 What is meant by index-linking?

11 List the organisations that can be useful sources of help and advice to a small business.

Assignment
Along the High Street

This assignment develops knowledge and understanding of the following elements:

RSA 11.1   Examine financial services providers

BTEC 12.1 Examine the financial services available to businesses

It supports development of the following core skills:

Communication 3.2, 3.4.

Your tasks

1 On an outline map of your nearest town, plot the position of all the providers of financial services. You should include:

- banks
- building societies
- insurance brokers

- insurance companies
- accountancy firms
- solicitors
- government agencies.

2 Prepare a list of all the services that each organisation represented in your town offers to its business customers.

3 Prepare an anaysis of your results which compares the range of services offered by each organisation, any cross-overs there may be in provision of those services, and any constraints there may be on each organisation.

Assignment
Small Business Advisory Unit

This assignment develops knowledge and understanding of the following elements:

RSA 11.1   Examine financial services providers

BTEC 12.1   Examine the financial services available to businesses

It supports development of the following core skills:
Communication 3.2, 3.4.

You are employed in the Research Department of your local Small Business Advisory Unit which is in the process of compiling a database of financial services available in your district. You have been asked to research some information to be added to the database concerning the terms and conditions that are required for various financial services.

Your tasks

1 Information is required about the terms and conditions applying to:
- a business loan
- business vehicle insurance
- a company pension scheme for 25 employees
- financial advice.

2 You should approach four of the following, and find out what terms and conditions apply, choosing a different service from each provider:
- a bank
- a building society
- an acountancy firm
- an investment/pensions fund manager
- a government agency
- an insurance broker.

The terms and conditions you require information about are:
- fees
- interest rates
- contractual arrangements
- security.

3 Collate your information in a form that can be entered into the database.

3 Consolidating business operations

This chapter examines the following:

- How business needs change as the business grows
- The type of financial services available to growing businesses
- How a business chooses between the providers and the services in the market

Survival and consolidation

The first 6 to 24 months of a business venture is known as the survival stage, when earning a living is the highest priority. At the end of this period, the business may seem to be quite different from that envisaged in the original business plan.

As a business enters the consolidation stage, it is important to take stock of the business achievements, and also to look at any weaknesses in the business. 'Good housekeeping' will become the priority rather than just earning a living, and good information systems are vital to ensure the management stays in control.

The Office of the Official Receiver lists the following factors as the most common reasons for a business to fail:

- not enough **capital**
- not selling enough
- bad management
- taking too much out of the business too early
- poor accounting
- lack of experience
- bad **debts**
- setting prices too low
- growing too quickly and running out of **cash**
- fraud
- operating costs getting out of hand
- poor supervision
- competition
- health problems of the owner.

How business needs change

As the business grows and changes, the need for financial services are going to change as well. During the consolidation stage of development these needs can be:

- the need for financial information
- the need to manage working capital
- the need for additional finance
- the need to manage risks
- the need for specialist advice.

It can be said that a business that is not growing is going backwards. It is almost impossible for a business to stand still in the long term. Generally, a business will grow over time, and many businesses will grow in a haphazard way, with problems being solved as they arise, and the management learning to cope as they go along.

Let us look at each of the needs of a business in some detail.

The need for financial information

The planning stages of setting up the business should have included the selection of a suitable record-keeping system. Earlier we looked at the criteria that a business could use to choose a suitable system. If that selection had been correct, the system should now be able to provide the information required for on-going monitoring of business progress. In particular, the business should be able to generate:

- cash flow monitoring
- periodic analysis of **debtors** and **creditors**
- production of profit and loss statements.

These pieces of information can then be used together to give an overall summary of the business situation at any given time, and can enable the management to keep control and take action before problems get out of hand.

Cash flow monitoring

Running out of ready cash can be one of the most common, and expensive, problems that a business can experience. The majority of businesses will arrange an overdraft facility with their bank to cover any short-term cash flow deficit. It is usually easy to arrange and relatively cheap. Problems arise, however, when the overdraft limit is unexpectedly exceeded, or when the facility is used for an extended period of time. Most banks charge punitive rates of interest to businesses who exceed agreed limits, and this should be avoided at all costs. In addition, running out of cash can have serious consequences for the business, even when, on paper, the business is making good profits. The following list of perils illustrates how important cash flow monitoring can be.

A business that runs out of cash may experience:

- excessive bank charges
- bounced cheques
- loss of credibility with suppliers
- loss of credit lines
- repossession of **assets**
- court action by creditors
- court action resulting in liquidation or **bankruptcy**.

A cash flow deficit can be caused by a number of factors, for example, an unexpected drop in sales volume, increased stockholding to allow for seasonal trade fluctuations (e.g. building up the stocks ready for Christmas sales) or unexpectedly high overheads in a particular month, but the most common is the business debtors not paying up on time.

While a cash flow deficit can be both expensive and potentially damaging to a business, it is also important to recognise when a cash flow surplus is likely to occur. Excessive cash within a business represents under-utilisation of an important asset, and the business may need to think about ways of making that asset work for the business rather that just sitting in the business bank account.

Understanding the difference between **cash** and **profit** is very important to any business. A profitable business can run out of cash, and an unprofitable business can be temporarily 'cash-rich'.

The profits of a business are calculated by taking the income from sales and deducting first the purchase cost of the goods (which calculates the gross profit) and secondly, deducting the expenses or overheads the business has incurred (to leave the nett profit).

The need to manage working capital

Earlier we defined working capital as the amount of money needed to pay your debts when they are due. In accounting terms this definition may be somewhat simplistic, and a better description might be

working **capital** = current **assets** - current **liabilities**

We have also discussed the consequences of a business running out of cash. Another way of describing this would be to say that a business had insufficient working capital. However it is phrased, the effects on the business are the same!

Judicious use of the information we talked about in the previous section can be developed into a strategy for managing working capital that can help a business ensure that it has the right amount of money, in the right place at the right time.

Credit management

Credit management covers a wide range of management techniques which aim to keep a close check on who owes the business money, and how much the business owes, and ensures that there is the right amount of money available to the business as and when it is required.

Monitoring creditors and debtors

The most useful way of monitoring debtors and creditors is to produce regular aged creditor and aged debtor analyses. These are produced by looking at the outstanding balances on each debtor and creditor account and creating an analysis of what is outstanding, and how long each item has been outstanding for. Many computerised accounting systems will produce this type of information automatically, but it may well be worth looking at the process in detail, as many small businesses will operate a manual system of accounting where this information has to be generated by the book-keeper. The process for creditor and debtor analysis is exactly the same.

Aged debtor analysis

Worked example ───────────────────────────────

The following example shows an account that has been taken from the Sales Ledger of ABC Ltd.

Maddocks Agricultural Services

Date	Item	DR	CR	Balance
1/6/X7	Balance brought down			296.42
2/6/X7	Invoice No. 259371	247.58		544.00
7/6/X7	Invoice No. 329876	156.92		700.92
20/6/X7	Invoice No. 419284	28.94		729.86
1/7/X7	Payment		296.42	433.44
5/7/X7	Invoice No. 500931	199.95		633.39
19/7/X7	Invoice No. 544920	429.70		1063.09
24/7/X7	Credit Note 3320		44.80	1018.29
1/8/X7	Payment		359.70	658.59

The first step in finding out how the balance is made up is to allocate all the payments and credit notes to the invoices to which they refer, and identify those invoices that are still outstanding.

Maddocks Agricultural Services

Date	Item	DR	CR	Balance
1/6/X7	Balance brought down			~~296.42~~
2/6/X7	Invoice No. 259371	~~247.58~~		544.00
7/6/X7	Invoice No. 329876	~~156.92~~		700.92
20/6/X7	Invoice No. 419284	28.94		729.86
1/7/X7	Payment		(296.42)	433.44
5/7/X7	Invoice No. 500931	199.95		633.39
19/7/X7	Invoice No. 544920	429.70		1063.09
24/7/X7	Credit Note 3320		(44.80)	1018.29
1/8/X7	Payment		(359.70)	658.59

We can now see which invoices are outstanding for payment, and how long they have been outstanding for. The next step is to record this information on an aged debtor analysis sheet as follows:

Customer	Credit limit	Balance	30 days	60 days	90 days
Maddocks	2,000.00	658.59	629.65	28.94	Nil

Having gone through all the accounts on a sales ledger, the aged debtor analysis would look like this.

Aged Debtor Analysis as at 1/8/X7

Customer	Credit limit	Current	30 days	60 days	90 days	90 days+
Maddocks	2,000.00	658.59	629.65	28.94	Nil	Nil
B. Johnson	2,000.00	429.16	429.16	Nil	329.05	Nil
Patel	500.00	225.00	225.00	Nil	Nil	Nil
Matthews	1,500.00	1,553.17	417.34	393.45	319.49	422.89

From this information, it is then possible to identify which customers need to be chased for payment.

Credit control

Identifying the outstanding amounts on the sales ledger is only half the story. Knowing who owes you money is not a great deal of use unless the business has some system in place to check on this information on a regular basis, and take action when necessary.

Nett monthly account Business credit transactions are usually conducted on a nett monthly account basis. While longer periods of credit are sometimes negotiated, it is usually expected that credit customers will pay their bills by the first of the month following the receipt of a monthly statement, i.e. transactions during the month of June will be shown on a statement which will reach the customer during the first week of July. Payment will be expected on 1 August. This will give the customer, on average, six weeks credit. Amounts outstanding during this period are classed as current debts. Should payment not be received on time, then it would be wise for the supplier to begin the credit control procedure.

Step 1
A reminder letter should be sent with the August statement, drawing the customer's attention to the overdue amount. This would usually be a gentle reminder, requesting payment within 14 days.

Step 2
If payment is not received by the next statement date, a letter should be sent requesting payment within seven days, and threatening court action if this is not received. It would be wise at this stage to review the customer's credit limit, with a view to refusing further orders if payment is not received.

Step 3
Action through the county court should be initiated if payment is not received within 14 days of the second letter being issued. The supplier should then put a stop on all further orders from the customer, and review the wisdom of continuing to offer credit terms to this customer.

While firm credit control is essential to the welfare of a business, it is also important to maintain good relationships with customers. It is therefore sensible for a business to be aware of circumstances that could legitimately affect the customer's will to pay, for example:

- Have credit notes been issued for all goods returned?
- Are credit notes being issued promptly?
- Is there any dispute over goods that have been damaged or do not meet with the customer's requirements in some way?
- Is there any other dispute that may affect the customer's willingness to pay, e.g. the amount of discount allowed, the incorrect computation of an invoice etc?

Activity ─────────────────────────────────────

The following aged debtor analysis has been produced by the Accounts Department of GGM Ltd. You have been asked by the Credit Control Manager to draft letters to the customers concerned, requesting payment of the outstanding amounts. You should draft letters that are suitable for each circumstance.

Aged Debtor Analysis for GGM Ltd as at 31/6/X8

Customer	Credit limit	Balance	30 days	60 days	90 days
Barton	2,000.00	240.01	229.05	10.96	Nil
Garten	1,000.00	1239.00	1239.00	Nil	Nil
Hasandra	3,000.00	2974.89	531.90	2320.56	106.50
Patel	2500.00	679.11	624.91	Nil	Nil

Invoice discounting

Invoice discounting is a debt purchase facility which offers to buy the outstanding debts to a company for up to 80 per cent of their invoice value, the balance, less any administration charge, being paid when the debtors pay. It is suitable for companies trading on credit terms with other businesses and is useful for avoiding a working capital deficit.

Factoring

This is a service which includes invoice discounting, but also has the facility to take over the sales ledger administration of a company. It is suitable for any business which sells to trade customers on credit, needs to increase its working capital and to ease the burden of administering its sales ledger. Bad debt protection can also be included in a package of services that can be tailor-made to the needs of the business.

Credit insurance

Credit insurance provides protection for a business concerned about the risk of non-payment by debtors through **insolvency** or protracted default. It can be taken out for a single project, for a specified period, or can cover the whole of a businesses turnover. It can provide up to 90 per cent replacement of liquid capital should a bad debt occur. It can also provide assessment of a potential customer's credit risk before a company enters into business with them. It is suitable for all businesses with trade debtors.

There may come a time when a working capital deficit is unavoidable, and a business must decide whether or not additional finance should be introduced to cover the shortfall. As previously discussed, an overdraft facility might be all that is required to see the business over a difficult time. If this is likely to be needed for more than a couple of months, then a business loan might be a more suitable solution to the problem. One of the problems with an overdraft is that the bank may recall the overdraft at any time, and this is most likely to happen if the business appears to the bank to be a deteriorating risk, and just at the moment when the business is in most need.

A business loan is a loan agreed for a fixed period of time, usually, but not always, at a fixed rate of interest. Repayment is usually by regular instalments of fixed amounts which makes **cash flow forecasting** simpler. Loan protection insurance can also be taken out to cover the owner of the business, partners or key employees in the event of accident, sickness or death. Alternative ways of introducing more capital will be discussed in the next section.

Case study

G M Cropthorne Ltd

Cropthorne's are unhappy about the way in which their debtors are controlled and have been considering subcontracting out their sales ledger to a local bank which provides services such as these to local businesses.

Activity

The following accounts have been extracted from the sales ledger of G M Cropthorne Ltd. Prepare an aged debtor analysis as at 1 November 19X6.

Wenham Engineering   Credit limit £3,000.00

Date	Item	DR	CR	Balance
1/9/X6	Balance brought down			429.67
4/9/X6	Invoice No. GB667	292.45		722.12
15/9/X6	Invoice No. GG2134	649.67		1371.79
20/9/X6	Credit Note CN221		56.91	1314.88
22/9/X6	Invoice No. GA2323	339.67		1654.55
1/10/X6	Payment		429.67	1224.88
7/10/X6	Invoice No. GC2232	543.97		1768.85
22/10/X6	Invoice No. GM4564	225.22		1994.07
1/11/X6	Payment		649.67	1344.40

Williams and Son   Credit limit £2,000.00

Date	Item	DR	CR	Balance
1/9/X6	Balance brought down			622.41
6/9/X6	Invoice No. GG6644	483.86		1106.27
15/9/X6	Credit Note CN1111		223.90	882.37
16/9/X6	Invoice No. GF5498	1259.49		2141.86
20/9/X6	Credit Note CN2961		189.70	1952.16
3/10/X6	Invoice No. GD4537	238.79		2190.95
15/10/X6	Invoice GD5185	564.81		2755.76
20/10/X6	Payment		662.41	2093.35

Jones Engineering Ltd   Credit limit £5,000.00

Date	Item	DR	CR	Balance
1/9/X6	Balance brought down			455.98
2/9/X6	Credit Note CN2211		24.90	431.08
3/9/X6l	nvoice No. GS2345	2830.67		3261.75
30/9/X6	Invoice No. GM5121	317.43		3579.18
1/10/X6	Payment		431.08	3148.10
10/10/X6	Invoice No. GB5472	598.90		3747.00
20/10/X6	Invoice No. GV2212	211.68		3958.68
1/11/X6	Payment		3138.10	820.58

Dhala, J B   Credit limit £3,000.00

Date	Item	DR	CR	Balance
1/9/X6	Balance brought down			621.94
2/9/X6	Invoice No. GS2562	338.20		960.14
4/9/X6	Invoice No. GM2210	298.71		1258.85
8/9/X6	Credit Note CN3122		56.31	1202.54
20/9/X6	Invoice No. GB2019	629.13		1831.67
4/10/X6	Payment		621.94	1209.73
6/10/X6	Invoice No. GV6191	712.91		1922.64
15/10/X6	Invoice No. GV9181	813.12		2735.76
23/10/X6	Invoice No. GV9332	723.90		3459.66
30/10/X6	Invoice No. GV9878	320.67		3780.33

Investigate the costs and feasibility of handing over the credit control to a local bank that provides such a service.

Assignment
G M Cropthorne Ltd

This assignment develops knowledge and understanding of the following elements:

RSA 11.1   Examine financial services providers

RSA 11.3   Recommend financial services for business organisations

BTEC 12.1   Examine the financial services available to businesses

BTEC 12.2   Investigate the financial services required by given businesses

BTEC 12.3   Select external providers of financial services to meet the needs of given businesses

It supports development of the following core skills:

Communication skills 3.2 and 3.4.

Your task

Prepare an oral report, including conclusions and recommendations for the board of G M Cropthorne Ltd, based on your findings from the activity.

Control of creditors

An aged creditor analysis should be produced from the purchase ledger in the same way as an aged debtor analysis. This can be used to ensure that:

- payments to creditors are made on time
- funds are available to pay creditors when due
- disputes are quickly taken up with suppliers
- expensive and damaging court action is avoided.

Managing a surplus

Spare cash lying around in a business is a wasted asset, which could be earning valuable interest and adding to the profits of the business. In addition many businesses like to put away sums for specific purposes such as **tax** or **VAT** payments. All of the **banks** and many of the **building societies** have interest-bearing accounts suitable for business use under these circumstances. Interest rates will reflect the rate of interest payable in the market generally, with higher rates being paid the longer a business is able to invest the money.

The market in interest bearing accounts is very wide and varied, but generally they fall into the following categories.

Free access accounts These accounts have no restriction on the timing of withdrawals. The interest rate is often progressive with the amount deposited and many have a cheque-book facility.

High interest accounts These accounts pay a higher rate of interest than the ordinary accounts, but access is normally restricted, either by the amount of notice that is required for withdrawal, (anything from 14-90 days), or by fixing the number of withdrawals that can be made during a period (usually a year). There is usually a minimum amount that must be deposited to open the account, which could be anything from £1,000 to £10,000, and should the amount in the account fall below a specified figure, the interest rate payable falls.

Fixed-term fixed interest accounts Many organisations offer accounts where money can be deposited for a fixed period of time and at a fixed interest rate. Periods can vary from one day to five years. These accounts are particularly useful during times when interest rates are high, but falling. The disadvantage is that it may not be possible to withdraw the money, at least not without paying a penalty, if circumstances within the business change and the end of the agreed period is a long way off.

Case study

> ### Marfell Ltd
>
> At the quarterly meeting of the Board of Directors of Marfell Ltd, the Finance Director presented the latest cash flow forecast to the Board. It showed a cash surplus of £17,500 for the quarter and it was decided that some of this money should be invested in an account to earn extra interest.
>
> As an assistant in the Finance Department, the Finance Director has asked you to investigate suitable investment accounts in which to put the money. He has supplied you with the following statement of expected calls that may have to be made on the money in the future. The current date is 1 July 19X4.
>
> | Amount £ | Date required | Purpose |
> |---|---|---|
> | 5,000 | 31.12.19X4 | Taxation |
> | 4,000 | 30.09.19X4 | VAT |
> | 2,000 | 10.09.19X4 | National Insurance |
> | 6,500 | Surplus to immediate requirements | |

Activity

You are required to investigate the investment opportunities offered by three different organisations: one bank, one building society and one other.

Assignment
Marfell Ltd

This assignment develops knowledge and understanding of the following elements:

RSA 11.1   Examine financial services providers
RSA 11.3   Recommend financial services for business organisations
BTEC 12.1   Examine the financial services available to businesses
BTEC 12.2   Investigate the financial services required by given businesses
BTEC 12.3   Select external providers of financial services to meet the needs of given businesses

It supports development of the following core skills:
Communication 3.2, 3.4.

Your task

Produce a brief report on services provided by the organisations you have investigated.

Your report should include the rate of interest that can be expected from each opportunity and any restrictions that may apply to withdrawals from the account. You should make recommendations as to which combination would be the most suitable to meet the company's needs, given the call that may have to be made on the cash.

The need for additional finance

As we have already seen, even a business with good management of its working capital and good on-paper profits can find that it needs additional funding. These needs can arise for a variety of reasons including:

- financing of an unusually large contract
- finance to cope with seasonal demand
- default on a major debt
- failure of an important piece of plant or equipment
- to take advantage of technological advances to improve efficiency and/or profitability.

Earlier, we found that we could classify financial needs into four main categories:

- short-term finance
- long-term finance
- finance of working capital
- finance of assets.

This classification remains useful when looking at a business in the consolidation stage of development.

Let us look at these again in detail, together with some other alternatives which could be available to a business at this stage of development.

Short-term finance

As a general rule, short-term finance is usual met in the following ways:

1 By an overdraft facility at the bank
2 By trade credit.

Overdraft facilities

We have discussed some of the advantages and disadvantages of a bank overdraft facility earlier in this chapter, but this facility remains one of the most useful sources of short-term finance, and one without which many businesses would find it difficult to manage. An overdraft is useful for financing:

- a short-term cash flow deficit
- increased stockholding to cope with seasonal demand
- increased stockholding or increased costs associated with an unusually large contract.

Although very useful, an overdraft should be used only as a short-term stop-gap. When an overdraft turns into a long-term part of the business finance, then it may well be sensible to look at other methods of finance or improved financial management.

Trade credit

As we have seen in the previous section, suppliers will supply goods on credit normally under the terms of nett monthly account. It is often possible, however, to negotiate longer terms of credit with suppliers. This can sometimes work out cheaper than an overdraft or loan facility, even when the supplier makes a charge for this service. Should a business need to increase its stock holding for some reason, it should approach the relevant suppliers for an increase in their credit limit to allow them to have a larger amount of goods on credit.

Long-term finance

Long-term finance is more suitable should the business require finance for more than a year, particularly when:

- new/replacement plant or equipment is required
- working-capital deficit becomes prolonged.

Bank loans

As we have discussed before when looking at financing for the individual, bank loans come in many different forms. They may have fixed or variable interest rates, and may have fixed or variable repayments. The interest charged will reflect the current bank lending rate and the degree of risk that the bank feels the loan represents.

Applying for a bank loan

When applying for a bank loan the business will have to supply the bank with detailed cash flow and profit forecasts. It may also be required to provide some security for the loan such as a charge on the business assets (similar to a mortgage if the business owns premises) or a share in the business equity (e.g. shares in a limited company). Small businesses that have insufficient resources to obtain a conventional loan may be able to overcome this difficulty through the Small Firms Loan Guarantee Scheme.

Small Firms Loan Guarantee Scheme

This scheme is a government-backed scheme which provides a guarantee of up to 70 per cent of an outstanding loan (85 per cent for 'established businesses'). Loans may range from £5,000 to £100,000, and a 'Capital repayment holiday' of up to two years is available on loans in excess of £30,000. Loans are repayable over two to seven years, and are available with fixed or variable interest rate options. The scheme enables qualifying small businesses to obtain funding when they are unable to benefit from conventional loans. The scheme can be used for virtually any purpose, so assisting the development of the business.

Activity

What would be the advantages to

a the lender
b the small business

of a loan under the Small Firms Loan Guarantee Scheme?

Hire purchase

A **hire purchase** agreement for a business is very similar to hire purchase agreements for individuals. It is particularly suitable for the purchase of assets such as equipment and motor vehicles. These loans are usually arranged through a **finance house** and allow the business to spread the cost over a longer period (typically two to five years). A hire purchase agreement differs from a business loan in that it is tied to the purchase of a particular item, the loan cannot be used for anything else. Also, the asset does not become the property of the business until the final payment has been made. Should the business default on the loan, the asset is returned to the lender.

Leasing

Under a lease, the business does not own the asset, but rents or leases it from the owner. Leasing packages are commonly available for large items of plant and equipment, and also for motor vehicles. In recent years a range of **leasing** packages have been developed, particularly for motor vehicles, whereby the business pays an initial deposit, followed by regular payments, and then at the end of the lease period, has the option to return the equipment to the lessor, or make a lump sum payment to obtain ownership of the equipment.

Sell and lease back

This is a fairly drastic measure, but one that a business may find useful in some circumstances. It involves the sale of a major asset which is then leased or rented back from the buyer. It will be available only in limited circumstances, with certain assets, but it can provide a useful way of relieving a cash flow deficit without adversely affecting the production capacity of a business.

Case study

Bolton Electrical Services Ltd

Bolton Electrical Services Ltd have decided to replace their ageing fleet of delivery vans. They need five new vans, and their preferred choice is something like a Ford Fiesta van. Their current fleet was purchased outright, but they are now interested in purchasing the new vans either through a leasing package, or through a hire purchase agreement.

Activity

They have asked you for some advice and you are required to investigate some possibilities for them.

Gather some information from your local van dealerships about the various hire purchase and leasing packages currently available. Contact two different organisations that offer either leasing or hire purchase contracts. Make a comparison between the two organisations which includes:

- the cost of the package
- the terms and conditions of the package
- the suitability for Bolton Electrical Ltd.

Assignment
Bolton Electrical Services Ltd

This assignment develops knowledge and understanding of the following elements:

RSA 11.1   Examine financial services providers

RSA 11.3   Recommend financial services for business organisations

BTEC 12.1   Examine the financial services available to businesses

BTEC 12.2   Investigate the financial services required by given businesses

BTEC 12.3   Select external providers of financial services to meet the needs of given businesses

It supports the development of the following core skills:
Communication 3.2, 3.4.

Your task

With reference to the case study, produce a short report for Bolton Electrical which details the following:

- the range of options available
- the comparative cost of each option
- the differences between leasing and hire purchase
- recommendations as to which option the company should adopt.

The need for specialist advice

As a business grows, and consequently becomes more complex, the need for specialist advice may also grow. The new business may get all the help and advice it needs from the small business advisor at the local bank, but in the consolidation stage it may be useful to cast the net a bit wider.

Accountants

All companies, most businesses and all entrepreneurs will need the services and advice of an accountant at some time. Deciding on which accountant, what size of firm and which services to buy are issues that all businesses will have to face at some stage. With accountancy firms coming in all shapes and sizes, it is important that a business is able to choose a firm that will be able to meet its needs.

The term 'accountant' does not necessarily mean that the person described has any formal accountancy qualifications, unless they are members of a recognised body. Membership of the **Institute of Chartered Accountants** or **Chartered Association of Certified Accountants** ensures that the person concerned has followed a required training course and has passed the necessary examinations to admit them to membership of that organisation. They are also required to comply with the Code of Practice of that organisation. A limited company wishing to engage an auditor must appoint someone who is a member of one of these bodies, which have been recognised by the Department of Trade.

In the early stages of a business, an accountant may only come on the scene at the end of the financial year when the business is producing its final accounts. As a business grows, it may well find it useful to avail itself of the many other services an accountant can offer, for example:

- adapting and developing recording systems
- developing costing structures
- identifying money making opportunities
- help in setting and monitoring targets and goals
- meeting legal obligations
- analysing investment opportunities
- analysing finance needs
- **auditing**
- taxation advice.

While in the early stages an independent accountancy firm may be engaged to provide these services, it may well be that in the consolidation stage, the business decides to employ a full-time accountant to work for the firm.

The only satisfactory way of choosing an accountancy firm to act for the business is by recommendation and by taking up references. It will then be necessary to enter into negotiations with the accountancy firm to decide whether the firm offers the services that the business needs, and which of those services it would be cost-effective for the business to buy. It may well be that the business would find it more cost effective to employ a Member of the Association of Accounting Technicians to work within the business preparing the books and final accounts, and buying in the specialist expertise management.

Activity

Working in groups of three, arrange an interview with a member of a local accountancy firm. (Names and addresses can be found in Yellow Pages). The purpose of the interview is to prepare a 'Day in the life of?' write-up for a careers pamphlet.

Before your interview you should prepare a list of suitable questions to ask which should include information on the following:

- the services offered by the firm
- the number of employees
- the number of partners
- the number of clients
- the type of clients (small businesses, large organisations etc).

Together with information on a typical day in the life of the person being interviewed.

Financial consultants

The term financial consultant covers a wide range of individuals and firms offering advice on all aspects of business. They may be accountants, banks or other professionals who have specialised in such areas as corporate and tax planning, raising venture capital or business organisation, and may offer financial consultancy as part of the range of services offered by their firm. A number of company agents marketing insurance and investment products now call themselves financial consultants offering a 'financial health check' as a preliminary way of identifying the financial needs of a business or an individual. As with insurance brokers and intermediaries, anyone offering investment advice must be registered with the **Personal Investments Authority** (PIA) or one of the self-regulatory organisations described on p. 74. However, anyone can set themselves up as a 'consultant' and the only way to be sure of the quality of service is to investigate their reputation in the business community, and to take up references. As a general rule, membership of one of the self-regulatory bodies should indicate a minimum standard of service, and compliance with the code of practice in operation for that organisation.

Solicitors

A business will find an increasing need for legal advice. A solicitor can help in the following areas:

- analysis and negotiation of business contracts
- purchase and transfer of property
- changing the organisational structure, e.g. from a sole trader to a **partnership** or a partnership to a limited company
- debt collection
- disputes with customers, suppliers, members of the public or employees.

As with accountants, a business may engage an independent firm of solicitors, or employ a full-time solicitor within the business.

The need to manage risks

The various types of insurance available to business has already been outlined, but as a business grows it will need to constantly review its insurance cover. The business needs may change because:

- asset values have increased
- there is greater reliance on the skill of particular staff
- risks may alter.

A new business may feel that engineering insurance or business interruption insurance for example, is too expensive for the benefit they offer in the early stages of a business, but during the consolidation stage of development, this type of insurance may become invaluable.

Activity ———————————————————————

1 Make a list of all the risks that might increase as a business grows.
2 Identify which of those risks could be covered by a standard policy from an insurance company.
3 Which of those risks could be classed as uninsurable?

Specialist insurance advice

As a business grows, the need for specialist insurance advice will appear, maybe for the first time. With insurance being such a complex and important issue to all businesses, the need for independent expert advice is paramount. With many different organisations actively marketing insurance services, it is important to be able to recognise and distinguish between truly independent advice and those organisations who are simply acting as marketing outlets and are therefore only representing a limited number of insurance companies.

Insurance companies

The major function of insurance companies is to pool the resources of many people to provide for unforeseen contingencies, or to provide financial assistance in the event of death. The money received in premiums is invested in a wide range of British Government and company securities, which provides a pool of funds from which claims may be met. Their experience in the field of investment makes them ideal intermediaries to act as managers for the investment of pension fund contributions.

The business of an insurance company is usually split into two sections, long-term insurance, which is life assurance and long-term sickness assurance, and general insurance, which deals with all the other areas, such as motor, property, personal and accident insurance.

The British insurance industry is a highly complex and specialised business, with more than twenty major British companies offering a wide range of services to business and personal customers.

Eagle Star, for example, offer over 100 different 'main line' highly specialised policies to large business customers, while Commercial Union offers a wide range of 'safety net' packages, which will include a combination of cover for building, contents, and specialised risks, for smaller businesses, tailor-made for the different trading sectors, e.g. hoteliers, retailers, motor traders, etc.

Actuaries

Actuaries provide detailed analysis of insurance needs and access to specialised insurance. Most businesses will not really have the need for this type of service except if they are thinking about creating a company pension scheme.

Independent intermediaries

Independent intermediaries are not registered brokers but are selling general insurance such as motor or building insurance. They are not obliged to have professional indemnity insurance (though many have, for their own protection) or to contribute to a compensation fund. They should, however, comply with the Code of Practice established by the **Association of British Insurers**.

Company agents

Company agents offer for sale the products of one company or group of companies. They will not therefore, be able to give advice in a wide range of options, but they will have in-depth knowledge of the products on offer by the companies they represent, and may sometimes be useful for negotiating special terms and conditions with an insurance company.

Under the Financial Services Act 1986 anyone offering advice on pensions or investment-type life insurance, such as endowment policies, must be registered with the Personal Investments Authority, which will take over some of the work done by **FIMBRA** and IMRO.

Choosing an insurance broker, intermediary or a company agent can be a hit-and-miss affair. So much will depend on the needs of the business concerned and the amount of research needed by the broker or intermediary. Many businesses will find all the cover they need from a 'safety net' package similar to the ones we encountered earlier in the chapter, while the needs of other businesses may be more specialised or complex.

In order to make a choice, it is necessary for the business to be clear about their business needs, both for the insurance they require, and about the services they need from their broker or intermediary.

Finding a broker or intermediary who will meet your very personal list of requirements will take some time and effort. However, a good starting point is the personal recommendation of someone in a similar line of business to yourself. Contacts with other business people through the various small business organisations or the local Round Table or Chamber of Trade could give a useful guide to who would be the best to deal with the needs of your business. Large organisations also use personal contacts and recommendations to make a shortlist of possible sources of advice.

There are a number of trade associations for independent financial advisors who will provide a list of members in a particular area. These associations include BIIBA (**British Insurance and Investment Brokers Association**), CIFA (Corporation of Independent Financial Advisors) NFIFA (**National Federation of Independent Financial Advisors**) and LIA (Life Assurance Association). Most of these organisations have Codes of Practice with which members are expected to comply, and while that is no guarantee that you will get a good service, it does improve your chances.

Most brokers and intermediaries will advertise in local business publications, or can be found in the local Yellow Pages.

Activity

Imagine that your business needs to appoint an insurance broker, intermediary or company agent for the first time. Working in groups of up to six, brainstorm the criteria that you would use to choose a suitable broker, intermediary or company agent to look after the insurance needs of your business.

Produce a checklist of criteria against which you can 'score' the services provided.

Contact BIIBA, NFIFA, CIFA and LIA and obtain a list of their members in your area. From the lists supplied, select two of each of the following:

- insurance brokers
- independent intermediaries
- company agents.

Make contact with them, and using the following information, obtain quotations for insurance.

Type of insurance required: Employers' liability
Type of business: Retail greengrocers
Number of employees: Five including spouse
Location: Your local High Street

Assignment
Selecting insurance advice

This assignment develops knowledge and understanding of the following elements:
RSA 11.1   Examine financial services providers
RSA 11.3   Recommend financial services for business organisations
BTEC 12.1   Examine the financial services available to businesses
BTEC 12.2   Investigate the financial services required by given businesses
BTEC 12.3   Select external providers of financial services to meet the needs of given businesses

It supports the development of the following core skills:
Communication 3.2, 3.4.

Using the checklist that you prepared during the brainstorming session, evaluate the service you received from each of the sources contacted and prepare an oral report for the rest of the group and your tutor on which one most nearly matched your ideal source of insurance advice.

Review your progress

1 What are the main reasons why businesses do not survive the consolidation stage of development?

2 What are the main ways in which business needs change as the business grows?

3 What are the consequences of a business failing to keep a check on its cash flow?

4 What is meant by 'working capital'?

5 Why would a business want to monitor its creditors and debtors on a regular basis?

6 What is the purpose of an aged debtor analysis?

7 What are the steps that a business can take to ensure that debts are paid when they are due?

8 What is the difference between factoring and invoice discounting?

9 Why would a company want to take out credit insurance?

10 How can taking out a business loan help a firm's cash flow?

11 Why would a firm want to control its payment of creditors?

12 Why is spare cash lying around in a business a wasted asset? What steps can a business take to make surplus cash work harder?

13 What would be the main types of long-term finance? What would be the most common use of this type of finance?

14 What is the Small Firms Loan Guarantee scheme?

15 What is 'sell and lease back'?

16 What type of advice can a solicitor give that could be called a 'financial service'?

17 What is the difference between an independent intermediary and a company agent?

Assignment
Taking stock

This assignment develops knowledge and understanding of the following elements:

RSA 11.1   Examine financial services providers

RSA 11.3   Recommend financial services for business organisations

BTEC 12.1   Examine the financial services available to businesses

BTEC 12.2   Investigate the financial services required by given businesses

BTEC 12.3   Select external providers of financial services to meet the needs of given businesses

It supports the development of the following core skills:
Communication 3.2, 3.4.

Joe and Maddy Kowalski have had a frantic two years since they set up their business importing and selling craft work from the third world. Selling mainly through mail order and a couple of high class retail outlets in Birmingham and London, they had been surprised by the amount of interest the craft work had generated. Maddy was particularly pleased with a range of Indonesian cottons that she had found on a recent trip, that were selling like hot cakes. In many cases, they could not get enough goods to satisfy the demand, and had spent much of the last two years flying around the world, arguing with local traders, bullying officials and travelling to some very isolated places to track down goods to satisfy the British public.

It came as a bit of a shock, therefore, when their accountant asked them to come in for a chat about their end of year figures.

'You really must pay more attention to "good housekeeping". Your accounts are a mess, your cash flow is perilous, and your organisation is chaotic. If you don't sort things out fairly quickly, you could find yourselves in real trouble.'

Sitting down to look at the business a few days later, Joe and Maddy had to agree. They had been so tied up with finding the goods to sell, they had spent very little time setting a solid foundation in the organisation at home.

The amount of bad debts they were incurring were rising beyond acceptable levels, and the business seemed to be growing too quickly, without the additional working capital to fund it. Their operational costs

77

seemed very high, certainly higher than they had anticipated, and poor supervision at home had meant that their organisation was not as efficient as it might have been.

They managed to identify a number of things that would help sort out their business.

1 They needed more financial information from their accounting system.
2 They needed to manage their working capital more effectively.
3 They needed additional finance.
4 They needed to manage risks more efficiently.
5 They needed some specialist advice.

Your task

Prepare a report for Joe and Maddy which identifies some of the weaknesses in their business organisation, and suggest ways in which those weaknesses may be overcome.

Your report should indicate which financial services would be useful for them, and which needs could be met internally, and which from external providers.

4 Going for growth

This chapter examines the following:

- How a business grows and develops
- How financial services providers can assist a business to grow
- The different services that can be provided

Going for growth

To begin with, it might be worth thinking about exactly what we mean by the growth of a business. It is not just a case of getting bigger. There are different measures of growth, and the type of expansion that a business undertakes will determine the path that it takes, the type of financing it needs, and its chances of success.

Throughout its life cycle, a business will have changing needs, which can be met in a number of different ways, either by outside financial institutions, such as **banks**, **building societies**, **insurance companies** and various providers of advice and specialist services, such as accountants and insurance brokers, or the needs may be met internally, from the resources of the business itself, or the resources of the owners.

We can measure the growth of business in a number of ways:

- increasing profits
- increased value of the assets of the business
- increased return on capital
- increased sales volume (turnover)
- a larger workforce
- higher levels of production.

Not all of these will be achieved at any one time. For example, higher production may be achieved with a smaller workforce, and increased sales volume does not automatically result in increased profits, so it really depends on the objectives of the business as to exactly which of these measures of growth are achieved during expansion.

There may come a time, however, when the management of a business decides to 'go for growth' over and above the normal evolutionary growth that all businesses should achieve in time.

Business growth can be achieved in a number of different ways:

- by expanding the market share
- by increased production
- by developing a new or unique product
- by extending the range of products
- by rationalisation to increase efficiency
- by introducing new technology
- by eliminating the competition.

Without a doubt, going for accelerated growth has its hazards for a business. It is unlikely that any growth can be achieved without:

- increased working capital requirements
- additional investment
- increased demands on the management skills of the business executives
- increased overheads and raw material costs
- thorough investigation and planning.

Case study

Evans Fabrications Ltd

Evans Fabrications Ltd manufacture fibreboard facia panels for the motor trade. They have a small pressings plant in the Welsh valleys, and sell mostly to a nearby car assembly plant. Their chief engineer has developed a new moulding that is capable of producing car child safety seats and has put a proposal to the Board of Directors that the seat be developed and marketed to increase the product range.

Evans have few competitors in the field of car facia panels, but the competition in the field of child safety seats is greater. However, with an estimated sales potential of some £300,000 per year, the senior management think that the idea is worth considering.

There is already some excess capacity in the moulding section that could be utilised for the new seats, but the spraying and finishing departments would have to have some additional equipment and staff, and some of the testing equipment would have to be modified.

Activity

1 Which of the measurements of growth are most likely to be affected should Evans decide to go ahead with the introduction of car safety seats to their range of products?
2 What are the main hazards that the Board of Directors should be aware of before making a final decision?
3 Where could financial services providers assist in ensuring that the expansions scheme is a success?

The time, effort and resources that would have to be put into going for accelerated growth have to be set against the potential increase in profits for the company in the long term. Following a nice idea because it looked like a good idea at the time is a recipe for disaster, which could seriously jeopardise the financial future of the business.

> 'For growth to be effective, it must be controlled and undertaken in planned stages as a result of determined management action.' (National Westminster Bank, 'Making the most of your business'.)

So how does a business go about achieving growth in a planned and controlled way?

Planning for growth

The process of planning for growth is very similar to the planning process of setting up a business for the first time, except that much of the information should be available from the existing company records. The business should have a great deal of information about its costs and markets from its existing operations which should take some of the guesswork out of planning expansion.

In planning for expansion, the business should go through the following stages:

- research the proposed expansion scheme in terms of its costs, market potential and profit potential.
- evaluate the profitability in the light of the time and resource required to put the project into operation.
- identify any structural changes that will need to be made to the organisation of the business or its management.
- produce a revised **cash flow forecast** and projected profit and loss statement.
- identify the additional funding that will be required.

Once the proposals have been fully formulated, and assuming that the whole idea is a viable one, the business will be ready to find the additional finance necessary to put the plan into operation.

Case study

Let us look again at Phillipa's business (see the case study on p. 34), two years on. Her predictions for her business have come true, and she has increased her sales considerably. Her increased purchasing power has meant that she has been able to reduce the costs of her raw materials. Her newly-installed computer system has produced the final accounts for the end of year two, which show a healthy profit.

Profit and Loss Account		
Sales		24,000
Less cost of sales		
Opening stock	600	
Plus purchases	8,500	
Less closing stock	750	8,350
Gross profit		15,650
Less expenses		
Rent	1,200	
Heat and light	1,000	
Van expenses	1,200	3,400
Nett profit		12,250

Let us imagine that Phillipa's business has been so successful that she has been approached by a major toy distributor who wishes to place a regular order for her toys. She is already at the limits of what she can produce herself and realises that she would have to make considerable changes in her operations in order to expand her business further.

Needless to say, she is very much in two minds about the contract, but at the same time, is excited about the prospect of turning her small business into something more profitable.

Activity

Knowing that you are studying Financial Services, Phillipa has approached you to help her get a clearer appreciation of how to approach the prospects of expansion of her business.

From the information contained in the case study, and from what we discovered in the earlier chapter, prepare a briefing for Phillipa which contains:

1 The changes she will need to make in her business in order to take on the extra work.
2 The risks she may be taking.
3 The financial services she could need to finance the expansion.
4 A plan of action she could use to evaluate her chances of success and find the information and help she will need.

Financing expansion

All the sources of finance mentioned in earlier chapters will be available to businesses wishing to expand their operations. To recap, these are:

- bank loans
- hire purchase
- leasing.

In addition to these, an established business may be able to draw on a wider source of finance than a business that is just starting up. As a general rule, however, businesses would be wise to ensure that not more than 50 per cent of the required finance should come from external sources. Most banks and other investors will want to see a good base of retained profits built up over a number of years of trading before agreeing to finance the expansion with a loan.

In the past, the market for financial services was straightforward. Most of the services supplied were very similar, and the interest rates paid or charged were more or less the same, no matter which organisation you approached. The range of products offered by the various institutions was limited and easy to understand, with little variation between organisations. The providers of services kept to their area of expertise, so if you wanted:

- a loan — you went to a finance house or bank
- a mortgage — you went to a building society
- a current account — you went to a bank
- to invest — you went to the savings bank (Trustee or National)
- an insurance policy — you went to an insurance company, maybe via an insurance broker.

The late 1990s finds the most competitive market for financial services ever. With profits under pressure for a number of years, the whole of the financial services sector is struggling to regain lost ground and to establish a solid base for the future. This has increased the blurring of the edges between one sector and another, with everyone trying to diversify and expand its market share. In this competitive atmosphere, providers of financial services have developed down two distinct tracks — integration and expansion of the services provided or increased specialisation in one area of expertise.

The integrated provider

The integrated provider of financial services aims to offer to the customer a complete package of services to meet his every need. This has the advantage of being able to sell a wide range of products to the customer, so that the customer comes to rely on the provider and will therefore be the first port of call for any future requirements.

The High Street banks are probably the best example of the provision of an integrated service. During the late 1970s and the early 1980s the banks began a series of diversifications, with the acquisition of insurance and finance house subsidiaries. This resulted in a corresponding development in their range of services, and reorganisation of their corporate finance sectors, into a team of specialists who could give greater support in handling the business of large corporate clients. The 1980s also saw the introduction of the business advisor, who has taken the place of the local bank manager in dealings with business customers.

The term 'Bancassurance' has been coined to describe these integrated providers who have expanded from their traditional banking base to provide a wide range of banking and insurance products to their customers.

Assignment
Banking services

This assignment develops knowledge and understanding of the following elements:
RSA 11.1   Examine financial services providers
BTEC 12.1   Examine the financial services available to businesses

It supports the development of the following core skills:
Communication 3.2, 3.4.

All the 'Big Four' High Street banks now produce packs for business customers giving details of the services provided.

Your tasks

1 Working in groups of three or four, obtain a business pack (called different things by each bank, but the contents are similar) which gives an outline of the various services on offer to businesses from two High Street banks.
2 Produce a 'family tree' of services to show the range of services on offer.
3 Make a note on the family tree of any subsidiary companies that are used to provide the services marketed through the business advisor.

The market for financial services is developing at an unprecedented rate, and change is the only certainty. So banks must develop and change their products to meet the changing needs of their business customers, and to maximise their market share.

Specialist providers

The other way to deal with increasing competition is to specialise in one particular area of financial services, and become so effective in that area that you provide a service that cannot be matched by an integrated provider. The **merchant banks** are good examples of organisations that have become increasingly specialised in the services they provide to their business customers.

There are today, some 100 institutions in the UK which call themselves merchant banks. They are financial institutions which provide specialist services to business including corporate finance, portfolio management, and other banking services.

While the range of services provided by merchant banks is variable from institution to institution, the following are examples of the type of services offered:

- portfolio management — the management of investments on behalf of pension funds, investment trusts, unit trusts and individuals.
- banking services — current, deposit and fixed-term deposit accounts, mainly for company customers.
- factoring
- hire purchase and leasing.

The merchant banks have also become involved with the international money or eurocurrency markets, and the international capital, or eurobond market. They often act for the UK and foreign companies and state enterprises to assist in the raising of medium and long-term finance.

During the last 20 years, all of the 'Big Four' clearing banks have bought interests in merchant banks, or have set up one of their own, for example, the one third share in Montague Trust, owners of Samuel Montague & Co, purchased by Midland Bank, and many of the corporate services of the clearing banks are offered through their merchant banking subsidiary.

Venture capital

The capital required for business expansion is often referred to as **venture capital**. The money can come from private individuals or from venture capital funds. There are currently over 100 venture capital funds in the UK, with money put in by pension funds, insurance companies, banks and investment trusts, regional development agencies and private individuals. They are generally looking for large or fast growing companies which could reach profits of £300,000 or more within three years. Finance is usually only offered to limited companies, and a share of the equity in the form of shares is usually taken as security for the loan. The fund will often want to appoint a director to the board, and a fee will be payable to him.

Some venture capital companies, however, will lend to smaller businesses and some specialise in helping people with innovative ideas start their business.

Private investors

These are a growing body of 'high net worth individuals' often referred to as 'Angels' who are prepared to provide money for risky ventures. They can be sometimes difficult to locate, although in recent years, a number of organisations have been set up to make this process easier.

LINC (Local Investment Networking Company)

These are run through the local enterprise agency network, and they try and put investors in touch with companies wanting funds. They send out a regular bulletin listing companies who are seeking funds, and charge the companies between £50 and £120 to appear in the bulletin. LINC will usually conduct an investigation of the company before it is listed in the bulletin, and would also want to investigate the scheme for which the funds were being sought.

Sometimes private investors will advertise directly in the Business to Business sections of daily newspapers such as the *Guardian*, *The Times*, the *Financial Times* and the *Sunday Times*.

Activity

From the back issues of the following newspapers, which should be available from the library, look at the Business to Business columns and find details of individuals wishing to offer venture capital:

- *Guardian*
- *The Times*
- *Sunday Times*
- *Financial Times*.

Forming a limited company

It may be that the owners of a business decide that they have grown to an extent that it would make sense to become a limited company. It must then decide whether it wants to be a private limited company (Ltd) or a public limited company (PLC). Under the 1980 Companies Act, a PLC is defined as a company with two or more directors, £50,000 issued share capital, of which at least 25 per cent must be fully paid (so a minimum of £12,500 is needed) and has a statement in the memorandum that it is a PLC. Any company which does not meet these criteria is a private company. In practice, the main difference between a public and a private limited company is that only a PLC may offer its shares and debentures to the public.

In order to form a limited company the business needs to register with the **Registrar of Companies**. It will need to submit:

1 A Memorandum of Association which states the name of the company, the location of the registered office, the objects of the company, its limited liability, its share capital and details of the shares. It needs to be signed by two or more people.
2 Articles of Association. This should contain the detailed rules about the management of the company. A standard format is set out in the Companies Act, or the business can devise its own.
3 Form 10 — Notification of First Directors and Secretary.
4 Form 12 — Declaration of Compliance
5 Registration fee (currently £50).

Once this has been done, a Certificate of Incorporation is issued, and the company can begin to trade.

Raising funds on the stock market

The main advantage of forming a public limited company is the possibility of obtaining access to additional funds through the **Stock Exchange** — that is, deciding to go public. Going public offers a path to further growth when other avenues such as bank finance have run their course, or access to other sources of funds may be restricted. It provides both a means to broadening the ownership of a company, and the ability to access the substantial pool of long-term capital available through the London markets. Companies are able to raise new capital by issuing shares for cash, and as a company grows and develops it may be able to raise additional funds in the markets both at home and overseas.

The stock market provides a mechanism for valuing and trading company securities. Further information about how the Stock Exchange works can be found in the Factfile.

The Official List

This is the oldest and most prestigious market for publicly quoted companies. Its origins go back to the early days of the stock market when an 'Official List' of securities suitable for trading was first kept and displayed on the floor of the market. Today, the majority of securities traded on the Exchange are companies that are 'listed'. The rules for entry to the Official List are set out in a booklet known as the 'Yellow Book'.

AIM

Introduced in 1996, AIM is intended to replace the Unlisted Securities Market, it is the third attempt by the Stock Exchange to create a market for smaller companies that do not meet the requirements for entry to the main listings. Both previous attempts have petered out after initial interest waned, and it is not clear how successful the latest attempt will be in giving smaller companies access to a market for their securities, and therefore to the additional funding that can be enjoyed by for companies on the main listing.

Methods of going public

There are three methods by which a company may choose to float shares on the stock market.

Offer for sale

Shares are offered by a company's sponsor to the public, inviting subscriptions both from institutional investors (such as insurance companies and pension funds) and the general public. The shares made available may be new shares offered for cash, or existing shares held by current shareholders. Normally the offer is underwritten. That means that the sponsor will ensure that all the shares are taken up even if the offer is undersubscribed, so that the company receives all the money that it is seeking to raise. The broker to the issue will make underwriting arrangements, mainly with institutional investors. Offers for sale are mandatory for offers greater than £30 million in size.

Application forms and the prospectus are advertised in the national press and are also available from outlets such as High Street banks. Offers for sale normally take place at a fixed price per share, that price being set immediately before the offer period, following discussions between the company and its advisors.

Occasionally, offers for sale are made by tender. In a tender offer shares are offered and underwritten at a minimum price and applicants may subscribe at any price at or above this level. A 'striking price' for all investors is determined on the basis of the applications submitted. Offers by tender have been used where it is difficult to set a price for the shares, maybe because there is no comparable company already listed to use as a benchmark to determine the company's value.

Placings

In a placing new shares, or the shares of existing shareholders, are offered to the public selectively. A company's sponsor or broker sells the shares to its own client base — typically investing institutions — finding purchasers with whom the shares are then placed.

Placings are particularly useful to smaller companies, partly because the costs are considerably lower than an offer for sale. There is less publicity and no wide-spread advertising.

Introductions

If a company already has a proportion of its share capital in public hands (25 per cent for the Official List and 10 per cent for AIM) the shares may be 'introduced' to the market. In an introduction, no shares are issued and no money is raised, it simply allows the shares of the company to be traded freely through the stock market. As there are no advertising or underwriting expenses, this is the cheapest and easiest way to float a company.

Activity

1 Search the back copies of the *Financial Times* and find a prospectus for a newly floated company.
2 From the share price listing, chart the changing price of the shares for that company over the two week period after the flotation. Plot the changing share price on a graph and comment on the changes that have occurred.

Mergers and take-overs

Sometimes a company may decide that the easiest way to expand the business is to take over or merge with another business. A take-over is where a company acquires a controlling interest in another company, but a merger or amalgamation does not require that all the shares are taken over. Often a 'holding company' is set up to control the original companies. There are several types of merger.

Vertical merger

In vertical mergers a business expands 'backwards' or 'forwards' to its markets. An example would be a shoe manufacturing company that bought a chain of shops.

Horizontal merger

In a horizontal merger the business expands and integrates with another business involved in the same activity, for example, a bank taking over smaller banks.

Mergers of diversification

Businesses frequently spread out into other fields to diversify their risks. One of the most interesting developments of the 1980s was the building societies buying estate agencies.

There are many reasons why a company would consider a merger or a take-over, but the two most important would be economies of scale and market domination, as we discussed at the beginning of the chapter.

Exporting

When investigating a path to growth many businesses decide to export their goods and services abroad. UK firms of all sizes successfully sell products and services overseas. Europe is now the UK's most important market with over 60 per cent of our export trade going to European Community and European Free Trade Area (EFTA) countries. With the completion of the single European market and strengthening of trade and economic relations, this percentage can be expected to rise considerably during the next decade.

Success in exporting can bring the company a wide range of benefits.

Economies of scale — larger runs and the reduction of spare capacity can enable firms to reduce their unit costs, and therefore make themselves more efficient.

Increased profit margins — profit margins on a wide range of goods can be equal to or higher than UK margins, particularly in the USA and in some parts of Europe. This allows firms to make a higher level of profit than they could by selling to the domestic market.

Spreading the risk — selling in several markets can help the business to adjust more easily to changes in the market-place. A decline in demand in one market, whether through recession or seasonal factors, can be offset by increases in another.

Enhanced reputation — selling overseas can boost the reputation of the business at home.

However, exporting has its downside as well, and any business could experience difficulties.

Export documentation

Although the single European market aims to standardise export documentation, firms can still experience difficulties ensuring that the right paperwork is obtained. These difficulties can increase dramatically in some areas of the world, particularly when things are compounded by language and cultural differences.

Market information

Obtaining reliable market information can also be difficult in some parts of the world, particularly those areas where a free market economy has only recently been introduced.

Finding business partners

Finding good distributors and agents in a foreign country can sometimes be problematic. It is not always possible to be physically present in another country for extended periods, and although large parts of the world can be contacted through fax and telecommunications, this cannot always be relied upon.

Payment delays and bad debts

Differences in language, culture and legal systems can make credit management a great deal more difficult.

Foreign currency management

Changes in currency values can disrupt trading agreements. A contract that appears to be profitable can become a liability six months later if unfavourable conditions exist in the world's currency markets.

Activity ───────────────────────────────────────

1 From the business pages of either the *Guardian, The Times*, or the *Independent*, note the values of the following currencies over a two week period:
   a Australian dollar
   b German mark
   c US dollar
   d Japanese yen
   e French franc.
2 Plot the values on a graph to show the changes that have occurred during the period.

───

In spite of the difficulties, the rewards for the individual business and the domestic economy can be large.

Fortunately, there is a wide range of help and advice available for firms that wish to export their goods and services. The importance to the national economy has been recognised and the Department of Trade and Industry is just one organisation that has developed a wide range of services to help the would-be exporter.

Services provided through the DTI

The Enterprise Initiative
The DTI Enterprise Initiative can provide a consultancy service on a wide range of topics. This can include advice on export marketing strategies.

Export Development Advisor

A national network of EDAs has been set up through the Chamber of Commerce network and financed by the DTI. The EDAs are all experienced export managers with industrial experience, who can provide advice and support to businesses who are either exporting for the first time, or who are trying to build on an existing exporting base.

Export marketing research scheme

This service is managed on behalf of the DTI by the Association of British Chambers of Commerce. It provides advice and financial support for businesses who have less than 200 employees to enable them to get foreign market research information.

Export representative service

The ERS scheme helps a business find the right representatives abroad, whether they wish to be represented by agents, distributors, importers or in some other way. It provides a comprehensive package of information and recommendations on potential overseas agents and distributors together with status reports on those considered to be suitable.

Overseas status report service

Impartial reports can be provided on overseas organisations which have been identified as suitable representatives or customers. The report will cover the organisation's trading interests and capabilities, the scope of its activities, what territory it covers, its warehousing and distribution facilities and its salesforce, its technical know-how and after sales service and any other agencies it already holds. Although the report will contain an indication of the financial status and resources or the organisation, it is not a formal credit rating.

New Products from Britain service

This service helps to promote innovative products of services by providing editors of magazines and journals with editorial material using information supplied by the exporter. It also provides a translation service into French, Spanish and Arabic.

Trade fair pamphleting scheme

This service provides space at selected overseas trade fairs and exhibitions for the display of company literature on a group stand.

Overseas Investment Enquiry service

This provides information about investment procedures in overseas markets. It can give details of relevant local legislation and information on professional advisors overseas. It will also provide credit ratings on potential investment partners.

Programme arranging service

After identifying possible business contact overseas, the PAS can assist in arranging a programme of visits, directions, names and addresses, and information on local etiquette, business practice and public holidays.

In-market help service

Local experts can devise a programme, accompany the visitor and de-brief him in order to help the business establish contacts with agents, distributors, professional advisers and other organisations.

Seminar organisation

This service is currently being piloted to UK trade associations and Chambers of Commerce who hold seminars overseas. The service includes advice, administration assistance, and trouble shooting.

The DTI is organised into eleven regional offices so that businesses can get support and advice on a local level. They also have 75 export promotions desks based in London, who can give information about specific countries or regions of the world.

Other services to exporters

Trade Bridge

Run in association with the London Chamber of Commerce and Industry, Trade Bridge provides business leads from a wide variety of sources, including the international network of Chambers of Commerce.

Sending and receiving money

SWIFT

The Society for Worldwide Interbank Financial Telecommunications (SWIFT) is a method of electronically sending money abroad using the interbank electronic network. Money can be directly transferred from a bank account in the UK to accounts anywhere in the world. The service is provided on two levels: urgent transfer, which is done in seconds; and standard transfer, which is an overnight service.

Foreign drafts

These are cheques drawn on a bank abroad. The bank will tell the foreign bank that the draft has been issued, and the beneficiary can then present the draft at the nominated bank to receive cash either in sterling or foreign currency. If it is presented to another bank, it is paid into their account like a cheque.

Foreign currency accounts

A currency account can be held in the UK or abroad, and operates in a similar way to an ordinary sterling current account. It can be used for paying and receiving payment, and helps to protect the business against currency fluctuations.

Eurocheques

Eurocheques are a method of paying for goods and services abroad from the normal business current account. They are accepted in over 40 European, Mediterranean and North African countries. They are limited to a clearance limit of around £700 and can be written in any currency, which is then converted to local currency at the prevailing rate, when the cheque is cleared. They can be used in conjunction with a Eurocheque guarantee card, which operates in the same way as a normal cheque guarantee card, and can also be used to draw cash from **ATM** dispensers abroad.

In addition, many organisations produce monthly or quarterly bulletins giving updated information about international trading situations, and highlighting companies who have been particularly successful or innovative.

Review your progress

1 What are the main measures of business growth?
2 Why cannot all of these be achieved at the same time?
3 What are the main ways of achieving business growth?
4 What are the main hazards of going for accelerated growth?
5 What are the main stages a business should go through to plan for growth?
6 What is 'venture capital'?
7 How would a company go about finding venture capital?
8 What is LINC?
9 What are the main documents required to form a Limited Company?
10 What are the three methods of going public?
11 What is the difference between a vertical and a horizontal merger?
12 What are mergers of diversification?
13 What are the main reasons why a business would wish to begin exporting its products?
14 What are the main difficulties of exporting? What services are provided by the DTI to help exporters?
15 What are the main ways of sending and receiving money abroad?

Assignment
Going public

This assignment develops knowledge and understanding of the following elements:
RSA 11.1   Examine financial services providers
BTEC 12.1   Examine the financial services available to businesses

It supports the development of the following core skills:
Communication 3.2, 3.4.

Nandla, Comer and Brown have been trading as a successful partnership for the last eight years, manufacturing computer hardware. They have decided that they would like to build a new factory and are keen to float the company on the stock market to raise capital for the expansion.

Before going ahead, they have engaged Wilmco Business consultants to conduct a feasibility study, and to sound out opinion.

Your task

You are a junior assistant to Mr Williams, a senior partner at Wilmco, who has asked you to prepare a briefing to introduce Messrs Nandla, Comer and Brown to the steps involved in becoming a PLC, and the various options available for floating a company on the stock market.

---

5 Public sector businesses

 This chapter examines the following:

- The need for financial services in the public sector
- How public services select the financial services they require

It is not just business organisations that have a need for financial services. Both state and local authority organisations have an increasing need for such services. In recent years, there has been a move away from centralised funding of services to a more devolved responsibility for managing **budgets**. This has caused a corresponding change in the need for financial services in public sector organisations.

This has affected these organisations in a number of different ways. For example:

- some organisations have more flexibility in acquiring loan capital
- the need has arisen for a specific skills within the organisation to manage the finances
- such things as insurance and banking facilities are now required whereas before these services were dealt with by the national or local authority organisation
- payroll, accounting and record keeping is now done at a local level, rather than centrally.

National state-run organisations

The National Health Service

The most dramatic change that has occurred in the National Health Service (NHS) over the last decade is the introduction of health service trusts to provide health care services to the community. Instead of being

provided by a local health authority, hospitals and ancillary care are now organised in the form of a local trust. Each trust is required to buy and sell its services to general practitioners (GPs) and other health trusts around the country.

Many GPs have become fundholding practices where they control their own budgets to buy medical services for their patients from any NHS trust. In theory, a GP can purchase health care from whichever trust can provide the most appropriate care for their patients, at the most reasonable cost. GPs are also free to provide services such as practice nurses and minor surgical procedures from their local surgeries, without the patients having to go to hospital, when this seems appropriate.

Activity

1 Find out how many GP practices in your area are fundholding practices and how many are not.
2 What do you think could be the advantages of being a fundholding practice?
3 What do you think could be the disadvantages of being a fundholding practice?

These changes have resulted in a greater need for financial services at a local level. Many of these services will be provided internally. For example, most fundholding GPs will have appointed a practice manager who not only oversees the budget, but also supervises the overall running of the practice.

Activity

1 What sort of functions do you think a practice manager would perform?
2 How would the performance of these duties help (or hinder) the service to patients?
3 How do you think management of a fundholding practice would have changed as a result of the new initiatives in the health service?
4 What types of financial services could a fundholding practice need that they would have found provided centrally before?
5 Which of these services could be provided by employing a practice manager, and which would be needed to be provided for from external services?

In the health trusts, many services that were once provided on a national level are now being required locally. Each department will now have a manager, responsible for the running of the department, and control of the budget.

Health trusts are also now encouraged to generate their own income wherever possible, which has resulted in managers looking closely at the use of their assets. In many cases, spare space in hospital buildings has been used to generate income and provide additional services for patients and their families by franchising out units to commercial enterprises such as newsagents, florists and catering businesses.

Activity

1 How do you think the roles and functions of health trust managers would have changed as a result of these additional activities now being undertaken by these organisations?
2 How would these additional activities affect the need for financial services?
3 Which of these financial services could be provided internally, and which would need an external provider?

Case study

The hospital concourse

The ground floor of the General Hospital in your local health trust has become rather dingy and dilapidated in recent years, providing a very unwelcoming approach for both patients and visitors to the hospital. In addition, the managers of the health trust are keen to improve their services to everyone who uses the hospital, but there is a severe shortage of cash to enable them to do anything much about it. One of the managers has suggested that it might be a useful exercise to consider leasing out space in the concourse to outside organisations who would provide services for the users of the hospital and provide some much needed income at the same time. Some money spent on dividing up the concourse into retail units of some kind and giving it a facelift could be offset against the money raised from leasing the units, and once the initial cost was recouped, income could be put into the general funds of the trust to improve patient care. The trust feels that the concourse would be large enough to accommodate six retail units without being too cramped, leaving the central area free for something like a refreshment area/cafe.

Activity

1 In groups of not more than four, brainstorm the sort of retail units that would be suitable for a hospital concourse.
2 Devise a list of criteria that could be used to narrow down the brainstorming list to the six most likely ideas.
3 Present your selection of the six retail units with your reasons for your choice.

Assignment
The hospital concourse

This assignment develops knowledge and understanding of the following elements:
BTEC 12.1   Examine the financial services available to businesses
BTEC 12.2   Investigate the financial services required by given businesses

It supports development of the following core skills:
Communication 3.2, 3.4

Your task

Having read the case study, 'The hospital concourse', prepare an action plan to assist the health trust to carry out a feasibility study on the idea of modifying the concourse into six retail units for lease. Your plan should include the results of your brainstorming exercise, together with a list of names and addresses of financial services providers whose services would be needed should the plan go ahead.

Dentists

As a result of a dispute over contracts, many dentists have withdrawn from the National Health Service and now only offer their services to private clients on a fee paying basis.

Activity

1 What difference do you think it would make to dentists in the way they organise their business now that they offer their services only to clients on a private basis?
2 How would their need for financial services be likely to change?

Privatisation

Many organisations previously run by the State have been privatised to some degree during the last 15 or so years, including many trading organisations, such as Austin Rover, British Gas and British Telecom.

The prison service

The first private prisons have now made their appearance into this country, where organisations such as Group 4 have built and run prisons which are leased to the Government. Prison officers and other employees are now employed by a private organisation instead of the State.

Activity

1 How would the privatisation of an organisation change its needs for financial services?
2 What type of services would now be needed?
3 How would the organisation go about choosing these new services?

Education

Schools

The introduction of local management of budgets and the extension of grant maintained schools through the 'opting out' system have again brought the need for financial services to a number of organisations that previously had their needs met centrally. Schools now have local management of their budgets bringing with them a need for new skills as well as new services. Many larger schools have employed a bursar to control the budget and expenditure. A number of smaller schools find it difficult to afford a specialist for these duties, and so it falls to the headteacher to fulfil these tasks as best they can.

Activity

1 What type of school do you attend? Is it grant-maintained, independent or local authority controlled?
2 Who controls the finances? Does the school employ a person specifically for these tasks, or does the head fulfil this role?
3 How many schools are there in your area of the same type as yours?

Colleges for further education

In 1993, further education colleges were removed from local authority control and are now public corporations which manage their own budgets received from the Further Education Funding Council. This has caused a great number of changes in the way colleges are organised. For example:

- they are now responsible for the maintenance of their buildings
- they have to have their own bank accounts
- they are responsible for their own insurance
- they control their own assets and can decide to buy or sell assets as needed
- they are responsible for their own payroll
- staff are employed directly rather than being employees of the County Council.

Some smaller colleges have continued to have close links with the local authority, but they now have to pay for the services they continue to use, while other larger establishments have decided to 'go it alone' and provide for the financial services they need from commercial organisations, or from their own resources.

Review your progess

1 What sort of changes have occurred in local authority organisations as a result of a move from centralised control to local control?
2 How have these changes altered the organisation's need for financial services?
3 What sort of services are likely to now be provided for by commercial organisations, and which are most likely to be met internally?
4 What does it mean when we say a general practitioner is a 'fundholding practice'?
5 How has the need for financial services changed as a result of becoming a fundholder?
6 What would be the advantages and disadvantages of employing a practice manager to run a fundholding practice?
7 What sort of changes would have to be made in the administration of schools and colleges as a result of local management of budgets?
8 How would their need for financial services change as result?

Assignment
The need for financial services in the public sector

This assignment develops knowledge and understanding of the following elements:

BTEC 12.1   Examine the financial services available to businesses

BTEC 12.2   Investigate the financial services required by given businesses

BTEC 12.3   Select external providers of financial services to meet the needs of given businesses

It supports the development of the following core skills:
Communication 3.2, 3.4.

Your tasks

1 Arrange an interview with the manager of a local fundholding general practitioner's practice, and with either the Principal of your college or the Headteacher of your school. Find out how the organisational changes have affected their need for financial services. You should identify which services are provided by external providers and which are now provided internally, by new specialist staff, or by existing staff having to learn new skills.

2 Produce a report on your findings which details:

   a the changes that have occurred in the organisations you have investigated

   b the financial services that are now required

   c how these financial services are provided (either internally or externally)

   d the similarities and the differences between the two organisations you have studied, and the way they have provided for the additional financial services now required.

6 Businesses in decline

This chapter examines the following:

- Why the owners of a business may decide not to continue trading
- How and why businesses run into difficulties
- What happens when a business becomes insolvent
- The financial services required to dissolve a business

Why the owners of a business may decide to cease trading

There are many reasons why the owners of a business may decide that the time has come to wind up their businesses and cease to trade. Perhaps the most obvious is if one or more members decides that they wish to retire. In the case of a sole trader or a partnership, this will often mean the end of the business in its current form. In the 1990s it is less common for a business to be passed on from father to son (or indeed to a daughter!) as it has been in previous generations, so a sole trader or a partnership may decide to simply sell the assets of the business and cease to trade on retirement.

Retirement

There are few formalities should a sole trader wish to retire. As the sole owner of the business, the sole trader simply puts the assets up for sale, pays off any creditors and takes the proceeds (less any liabilities there might be for capital gains tax). The process for ending a partnership is usually contained in the partnership deed, and unless the deed says otherwise, the retirement of one partner will normally bring the partnership to an end. It is then just a case of selling the assets and dividing the proceeds in the manner agreed in the deed. If there are a number of employees to consider, then the owners of the business will probably wish to sell the business as a going concern, to enable them to have the chance of continuing in employment with the new owners. It is also possible that the business may be worth more by selling it as a going concern, if there is valuable **goodwill** associated with it.

Changes in owners direction

The owners of a business may decide to cease trading because of other opportunities that become available. It may be that the owner decides to take up employment with another firm, either because of increased opportunities, or because the business is earning insufficient money to provide an adequate return on capital or to compensate the owner for the amount of time and effort that is involved with running their own business.

Changes in market structure

Changes in demand for a product or service may lead the owners of a business to divert their energies into other areas, which may result in the original business ceasing to trade, at least in the short term.

Bankruptcies and insolvency

In previous chapters we have discussed the reasons why a business may be unable to pay its **debts** and become **insolvent**, or the owners of the business may become **bankrupt**. A business becomes insolvent when its assets are no longer worth more than the business liabilities. The following diagrams show the steep rise in the number of insolvencies and bankruptcies that have occurred in recent years.

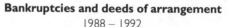

Bankruptcies and deeds of arrangement
1988 – 1992

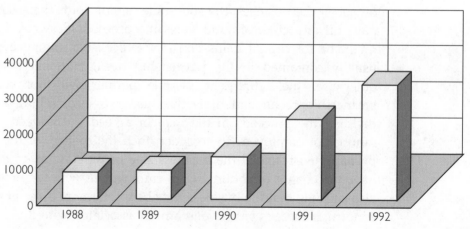

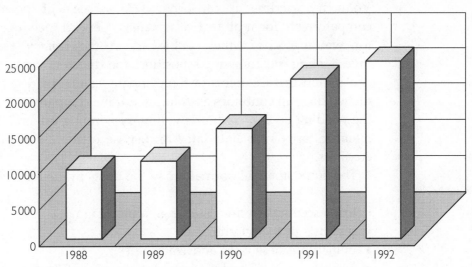

Company insolvencies
1988 – 1992

Research has shown that the warning signs of business failure can often be seen long before the business actually becomes insolvent. Among other things, studies have pinpointed the following factors which contribute to business failure:

- the owners of the business do not take advice
- one person holds the post of both managing director and chairman
- the Board of Directors do not take an active interest in the running of the business
- the skills of the business are unbalanced
- there is no budget, cash flow forecast or costing system
- the business is unable to respond to change.

Activity

1 Why do you think that insolvency and bankruptcy have been on the increase during the last ten years?
2 Find out the latest annual figures, and compare them with the graph above.
3 What measures would help a new business avoid being unable to pay their debts?

Once a company is insolvent, then it has to be wound up. This can be done either voluntarily or compulsorily.

Voluntary winding up

Voluntary winding up can occur if 75 per cent of the members of the company vote for it at an Extraordinary General meeting. The resolution for winding up is then published in the *London Gazette*. If, after investigating the company's position, the directors can make a statutory declaration that the debts of the company can be paid within 12 months, the winding up continues as voluntary. If the company is unable to do this, the winding up is a creditor's voluntary winding up, and in this case, the members appoint a liquidator to dispose of the assets on behalf of the creditors.

The liquidator will normally pay the debts in the following order:

- loans secured specific asset, e.g., a mortgage
- the costs of the winding up
- unified business rates and water rates
- income tax, VAT and National Insurance contributions
- wages and salaries
- secured loans with a floating charge (i.e. not secured on one particular asset)
- ordinary trade creditors
- shareholders.

Compulsory winding up

A creditor or a bank can apply to the court for a compulsory winding up if the company cannot pay its debts. The court will appoint a liquidator who is usually the Official Receiver. The secretary or director of the company must then provide a statement of assets and liabilities of the company. The liquidator will then pay the debts in the same order as for a voluntary winding up.

Bankruptcy

A sole trader or a member of a partnership can be made bankrupt if they owe more than £750 to a creditor who decides to apply to the courts for a bankruptcy order. Once the order has been made, the court may continue with the bankruptcy even if the outstanding amount is paid, if the court is of the opinion that the individual has other debts that cannot be paid.

Once an order has been made, the courts will appoint a liquidator who will hold a creditors' meeting, and dispose of the assets and pay the debts as described in voluntary winding up of a company. This will extend not only to the business assets, but the personal assets as well.

Voluntary arrangements

A business which is in financial difficulties may be able to avoid winding up or bankruptcy by coming to a formal arrangement with the creditors. This could either be to pay off the amount owed in instalments, or to offer to pay a certain amount in the pound in final settlement of the debts. As trade creditors are a long way down the list when debts are paid through bankruptcy or winding up, it may be in their interests to accept such a deal, if otherwise they would come out with a lot less, or maybe nothing at all.

The steep rise in insolvency and bankruptcy during the late 1980s and early 1990s has to be set against the rising numbers of people who have decided, for one reason or another, to become self-employed during the same period. In a large number of cases, the move to self-employment came as a result of redundancy, and the large 'golden hand-shake' which has enabled many people to realise their dream of starting their own business. While many have been successful — particularly if they had 'transferable skills' which could be 'sold', for example, by setting up a consultancy — a large number of businesses set up in this way have failed. Research has shown that only 20 out of 100 businesses started with redundancy payments will still be trading after six years.

Case study

A dream come true?

On 1 July 1992, John Freer's dream came true. After 15 years as a telephone engineer he was free. In one of the largest 'downsizing' operations in British corporate history, he and 19,479 fellow staff at BT accepted voluntary redundancy. They left on the same day. He had a £17,000 cheque in his back pocket and a huge sense of relief. 'When I woke up the next day, I thought "Magic". I was full of enthusiasm. I was signed up on a government enterprise scheme at £30 a week. I was going to set up my own business, double glazing. Everything seemed great.'

Once reality hit him after he left BT, disillusionment soon set in. Living in Middlesbrough, with a son aged five and an eight year-old daughter, the prospects quickly turned grim. 'The double glazing didn't work out. There were so many blokes doing it. It wasn't possible to undercut them.' After six months he was back on the dole, where he stayed until early in 1995.

Source: *Independent*, Friday, 8 December 1995

Activity

John Freer managed to avoid bankruptcy with his new business, but many new businesses do not.

1 Where do you think John went wrong with his business? What were the main reasons that his business failed?
2 Prepare a short report which explains the steps John could have taken to ensure that the new business he was starting had a better chance of survival.
3 How could financial services have helped in making his new business a success?

Even well-planned business ventures will from time to time come unstuck leaving the owners with huge debts. Sometimes, the reasons for failure are totally outside the owners' control. The collapse of a major business in an area will often force many other smaller businesses into liquidation as they in turn find that they are no longer able to pay their debts.

For a number of years now, business and consumer organisations have been pressing for legislation that will force businesses to pay their bills on time and thus ease the cash flow difficulties of smaller businesses; but while the economic and trading position remains uncertain, it seems unlikely that big business will concede to demands that it does so.

The banks have not always been the friend to small businesses that their publicity would have everyone believe. Many small businesses have run into difficulties because their bankers have changed the terms and conditions of loans or called in overdrafts at the first sign of difficulties. Small business organisations have accused the banks of 'cutting and running' at the first sign of difficulties, pushing small businesses into liquidation, often unnecessarily.

STINK-BOMBER BANNED FROM BARCLAYS

'THE BANK RUINED MY BUSINESS'

BANK FOUND GUILTY OF GIVING 'BAD ADVICE'

BANK MUST PAY COMPENSATION FOR RUINED BUSINESS

1 Using a CD-ROM or a Clover Index, research a selection of incidents where banks have been accused of damaging small businesses by what has been termed their 'heavy handed approach' to businesses in difficulties.
2 Prepare a short report on why you think the banks have operated in the way they have in these cases.
3 Arrange an interview with the owner of a small business, and find out what the relationship has been with their bank. Find out how the bank has helped or hindered the progress of the business in the last five years or so. Has the relationship with the bank changed during that period?
4 What have the banks done to improve the relationship with their business customers as a result of the bad publicity they have received recently?

No matter what the reason is for a business folding, the owners of a business will require help and assistance in realising the full value of their assets, and in some ways this brings us back full cycle to where we began this investigation on the financial services required by business. In Chapter 2 we looked at the services required to start a business, and in that we looked at the services required if someone decided to buy a going concern. In realising the assets of a business, the owners will be completing the cycle, for without people deciding to retire or cease trading, there would be no businesses on the market for aspiring entrepreneurs to buy. Someone selling a business would use the same range of services as someone buying a business, for example:

- estate agents
- solicitors
- accountants
- financial advisors.

Similarly someone retiring from a business would need help and advice on how to invest the capital they had realised to provide them with an income during their retirement, so they would need the range of personal services we examined in Chapter 1 such as:

- investment consultants
- building societies
- insurance companies.

The market for financial services is a highly complex and competitive one, where companies are constantly trying to tailor their products to the ever-changing needs of both their business and their personal customers. In doing so, they sometimes get things wrong, as in the recent cases involving advice given to clients concerning their pension requirements has illustrated. However, in spite of the many problems and difficulties the industry faces in our rapidly changing economy, there can be no doubt that this industry is a vital one which contributes greatly to our economy generally, and specifically to the continuing development of the country's business community.

Review your progress

1 What are the main reasons why the owners of a business may decide to cease trading?

2 What is the difference between bankruptcy and insolvency?

3 What are the main warning signs that a business may be running into trouble?

4 How does voluntary winding up of a business differ from compulsory winding up?

5 In what order will a liquidator normally pay the debts of a business?

6 What steps could the owners of a business take to avoid being made bankrupt?

7 What are the consequences of bankruptcy on a sole trader?

8 What is a voluntary arrangement?

9 Some reasons for insolvency are outside the owners' control. In what situation could a business find that this happens?

10 Which financial services are the owners of a business most likely to require in order to liquidate the assets of a business?

Assignment
Waiving or drowning?

This assignment develops knowledge and understanding of the following elements:
RSA 11.1   Examine financial services providers
BTEC 12.1   Examine the financial services available to businesses

It supports the development of the following core skills:
Communication 3.2, 3.4.

Andy Kapur was sitting in the pub one Saturday night when he spotted an old friend John Edwards, who had taken voluntary redundancy from the firm where he worked about 12 months ago, with the idea of setting up in business on his own. Stopping for a chat over his pint, Andy was surprised at the change in John, who looked ten years older than when he had last seen him, and definitely harrassed. Wondering if he should ask how the new business was going, John brought up the subject a couple of minutes later.

'I'm not really sure I made the right decision, you know Andy. Life has been really tough in the last 12 months. Just as we seemed to be turning the corner, Matthews Engineering goes bust, and I find myself right in the cart'.

'How's that affected you, John?' asked Andy.

'I'll tell you how! They owed me £15,500 that's how. Now I don't know what to do. The bank is pressing me to repay my overdraft, and while I could just about manage that, the rest of the creditors would be down on me in a fortnight. I tell you Andy, I'm facing losing everything. You've had some experience of this sort of thing, with your business studies course and everything, what do you reckon I should do?'

Andy left the pub having promised John to see if he could come up with some ideas that might help him solve some of his business problems.

Your task

Prepare a list of names and addresses that John could contact to seek advice on his business difficulties.

Factfile

The factfile is an alphabetical index which is intended to be used in conjunction with the preceding chapters, which amplifies and extends the background information contained in the body of the book.

A

ABBEY NATIONAL PLC

Although Abbey National Building Society only came into being in 1944 as the result of the amalgamation of the Abbey Road Society and the National Building Society, the company can trace its history back over 100 years to a period of radical political and economic reform. The National was established in 1849 at a time when voting rights were restricted to men who owned 40 shillings worth of land, so only one householder in six had the right to vote. The National offered a man a way to get the required value of land and also aimed, in the words of the first annual report 'to provide a man with the surest Bank for his Savings and the most profitable investment for his Capital'. By the 1880s the National was one of the largest permanent societies.

Meanwhile, in 1874 some members of a Free Church in St John's Wood, London, met in the chapel schoolroom to form the Abbey Road Building

Society with the aim of buying their own homes and having a 'trustworthy medium to invest savings'. From such small beginnings, the society grew rapidly, and by 1927 total assets had reached £10 million. The prosperous society moved into grand new premises at Abbey House, Baker Street, at 221b to be precise, the home of fictional detective Sherlock Holmes. In fact, 221b Baker Street did not exist when Sir Arthur Conan Doyle wrote his famous crime stories in the late nineteenth century, but from the time the Abbey Road Society opened in 1932, letters addressed to Holmes began to arrive, and continue to arrive by the sackful today.

The merger of the two societies was partly a response to the grave housing shortage created by the Second World War. They decided it was more valuable to co-operate than to compete on funding the reconstruction of houses destroyed by the war. Large as the new society was, it was still based on the share account, one which allowed members interest on their money, while also being able to withdraw at short notice.

From the early 1960s Abbey National began to develop its range of accounts, devise new services, and open hundreds of local branches throughout the UK. The base share account eventually expanded into a wide variety of accounts offering a range of interest rates and withdrawal facilities. By the 1980s investors were holding the basic share account, the Higher Interest, Seven Day, Cheque Save, Bond Share, Build-up Share and Junior Saver accounts as well as being introduced to pension plans and Save as You Earn (SAYE) schemes. In 1987 Abbey National launched a network of automated teller machines (ATMs) which have spread throughout Britain, giving account holders 24-hour access to their money through the Link network.

In 1987, after the Building Societies Act was passed, Abbey National decided to convert to a PLC. With the relaxation of the restrictions on the banks during the 1980s, Abbey had experienced heavy competition from the banks in the once protected home-loans market, and began to question how well they would survive as a mutual, unable to diversify beyond a limited range of activities. It was felt that by converting to company status, the Society could raise substantial share capital, enhancing its competitive power and its ability to diversify. Abbey National PLC was launched on Wednesday, 1 July 1989. Since that time, Abbey National has diversified its activities into Estate Agency, unsecured loans and in order to provide a service to business, Abbey National Financial Services Ltd was created as a wholly-owned subsidiary, providing pension advice, corporate tax planning services and insurance services.

ACCOUNT

The word account is used in a number of different contexts, but is usually meant to refer to a means of keeping track of money. In the financial accounting sense, an account is a page in the ledger where credit transactions with a particular customer or supplier are recorded. A summary of these accounts will enable the business to determine who owes it money, and to whom money is owed.

In terms of banks and building societies, accounts record the deposits and withdrawals a customer makes over a period of time, and interest due on deposits is calculated.

ACCOUNTANT

The term accountant does not necessarily mean that a person has any formal accountancy qualifications, so it is important for a business to accretion the qualifications of the person they wish to employ. Membership of one of the recognised associations will ensure that the individual has passed the required examinations to a satisfactory standard, and also will be bound by the code of practice and ethical standards set down by that association. In the UK, there are three main associations for people in this line of work: the Association of Accounting Technicians, the Institute of Chartered Accountants, or the Chartered Association of Certified Accountants.

AGENT

An agent is the term used to describe the relationship between one business and another when conducted via a third party — the third party being the agent. The legal standing of an agent is a complicated area of law, but for general business purposes, it is important to understand which business the agent is acting on behalf of. This is because only the business that is represented by the agent will be bound in law by any agreement the agent makes. If, therefore, you think that the agent is acting on behalf of a company, whereas they are really acting for you, the contracts that you think you have made, and the terms and conditions you have agreed to, may not be binding on the other firm.

ANNUITY

An annuity is a special type of insurance policy usually bought with a lump sum, to provide the insured person with either a lump sum at a predetermined date, or an income over a specific period. Annuities are often used to provide for specific events, such as school fees, a child's wedding, or to provide an income in old age.

ARTICLES OF ASSOCIATION

The Articles of Association contain the rules and regulations for the internal management of a company. A standard format is set out in the Companies Act, which may be adopted when the company is formed, or the company may devise its own. Copies of the standard articles can be purchased from law stationers.

ASSETS

Assets are items that a business has use of over a period of time. They are commonly classified as either fixed or current assets.

Fixed assets are items that a business will continue to use for a long period of time, such as building, premises, plant and machinery or motor vehicles.

Current assets are items that change in value more rapidly, such as cash at bank and in hand, stock, or debtors.

Liquid assets are those assets which can be readily turned into cash, such as stock or debtors.

ASSOCIATION OF BRITISH INSURERS

The association is the trade association of insurance companies. Their address is: ABI, 51 Gresham Street, London, EC2 7HQ.

ATMs

The Automated Teller Machine (or hole in the wall) has become a common feature of the High Street in the last 20 years. Designed to alleviate congestion at bank and building society counters, it also allows customers access to their accounts outside normal banking hours, when they may withdraw cash, conduct balance inquiries, transfer funds between accounts and make deposits without entering the premises. Customers may also access their accounts while abroad. Initially, ATMs were sited outside bank and building society premises, but there has been a trend in recent years to install them at such places as railway and bus stations, out-of-town shopping complexes and airports. The banks and building societies operate two separate systems, and some may make an additional charge for using an ATM belonging to another bank or building society.

AUDITING

Auditing of the accounts means that an independent body certifies that the accounts are a true record of the business's transactions during an accounting period. A limited company must have the accounts audited annually by a member of a body recognised by the Department of Trade as auditing bodies. However, many businesses will conduct an audit on a regular basis for a number of reasons:

- to satisfy the Inland Revenue that profit figures declared are accurate
- to support an application for a loan or mortgage
- to prevent or uncover fraud.

B

BALANCE SHEET

A balance sheet is the statement of assets and liabilities of a business at any one moment in time. So long as a business is trading, the value of its assets and liabilities will continually change, so the balance sheet is like a snapshot of one particular time in the life of that business. A balance sheet is usually produced at the end of each accounting period (usually once per year) but it can be prepared at any time. It is a useful document, that can be used to calculate the business performance in terms of its liquidity, its efficiency and its profitability. Comparisons with previous years' balance sheets can give both management and potential investors a valuable insight into the trading position of the business.

BANK

When you first think of a bank, most people will think of the 'Big Four' High Street banks — Barclays, Midland, National Westminster and Lloyds. These, together with the Royal Bank of Scotland, TSB and

Girobank (now Alliance & Leicester Girobank) are known as the retail or clearing banks.

The origins of British banking go back in history to the mid-seventeenth century. Prior to that date, city merchants and other wealthy people kept their valuables at the Royal Mint, which was then situated in the Tower of London. This ceased to be a safe place for deposits when, in 1640, King Charles I seized £200,000 of bullion belonging to the merchants to finance the army that Parliament had refused to grant him the cash for. The merchants of London then began to search for an alternative safe deposit for their valuables. The London goldsmiths had, because of their trade, excellent strongrooms, so they became the obvious choice for the wealthy of the city to store their valuables. The goldsmiths began to issue receipts for the deposits, and it was soon found that their receipts were being passed from one trader to another in settlement of debts. This saved the trader the trouble of going to the goldsmith, withdrawing his deposit and then handing it over to his creditor — it was much simpler to hand over the receipts. To make this process easier, the goldsmiths began to issue receipts in different denominations, and to make them payable to bearer, so that the title would 'pass by delivery'. This system is the origin of the modern bank note, and is the reason why current bank notes still have the words 'I promise to pay the bearer on demand the sum of?' written on them.

The goldsmiths began to concentrate on the banking side of their business and soon found that, at any one time, only a small proportion of the coins they were holding for safe-keeping would be required to meet the demands for payment of their receipts. They began to lend the surplus monies and to charge interest for doing so. By 1677 there were 44 goldsmith-bankers operating in London.

The communication and transport difficulties of the seventeenth and eighteenth century effectively prevented the goldsmiths or the Bank of England from opening branches in the provincial cities. It was left to the wealthy merchants to found banks in their own locality. The merchants added banking to their already established trade in the same way as the London goldsmiths had, and the number of country banks grew rapidly particularly during the second half of the eighteenth century.

Most banks printed their own bank notes, and a few their own coinage, until that was prohibited in 1812. The major problem of the country banks was the fact that the 1709 Act limited the size of banks wanting to issue their own bank notes to a maximum of six partners. This meant that they were unable to set up a branch network or to spread the risks. There was often a lack of professional banking expertise and sometimes a conflict of interest in decision making, as banking was very much a side line to the merchants' other activities.

These problems resulted in a severe financial crisis which led to the failure of 90 private banks during 1825. In 1826 the Government passed legislation to stabilise the banking system which allowed the opening of joint stock banks outside a radius of 65 miles from London. In addition, the Bank of England was persuaded to set up branches in Gloucester (1826), Birmingham, Leeds, Exeter, Liverpool and Bristol (1827), Newcastle upon Tyne (1928), Norwich and Hull (1829) and Plymouth and Portsmouth (1834).

The first joint-stock bank was opened in Lancaster in 1826, and by 1833 nearly 50 joint-stock banks had been established around the country.

By 1844 there were 105 joint-stock banks, and few were formed after this date. The decline of the private bank set in and by 1900 the private bank was virtually extinct. The joint-stock banks began to merge, and the branch network began to be developed. An Act of Parliament in 1862 allowed the company banks to have limited liability, and this opened the way to the establishment of the large banks that we know today.

The Bills of Exchange Act 1882 contained the provision for crossed cheques to be issued and gave protection to the banks and their customers against loss through theft and fraud, which increased the usefulness of cheques and gave banks greater scope for developing current accounts. A series of amalgamations between 1890 and 1914 brought most commercial banking into the hands of sixteen banks, and by 1918 this number was reduced to five large banks, and a handful of smaller banks.

BANK ACCOUNT

When we talk of a bank account, we are usually referring to a current (or cheque) account at a bank or a building society. In recent years, the types of accounts that can be opened at a bank or a building society has expanded enormously as the industry attempts to meet the needs of an ever widening customer profile. To meet the needs of a changing client group, it is now possible to open a variety of interest bearing and non-interest bearing accounts, some with an automatic overdraft facility, and some with cheque books, or alternatively just with an ATM card with which to operate it.

BANK BALANCE

The amount of money held in an account at the bank.

THE BANK OF ENGLAND

In 1694 a group of wealthy London merchants and financiers founded the Bank of England. It was established under royal charter with a capital of £1.2m, as a 'joint-stock company', similar in standing to a modern day limited company. The new bank was given the right to issue bank notes, and in 1709, the Bank of England Act renewing the Bank's charter gave it a virtual monopoly of joint-stock banking which was to last until 1826.

In 1715, the bank began to act as an agent for the issue and management of British Government loans, and during the first half of the eighteenth century the Bank of England became the banker to the principal Government departments, a role which it still holds today.

In 1770, the London goldsmith-bankers abandoned the issuing of their own bank notes in favour of Bank of England notes. This withdrawal brought about an increased use of cheques in London, and in 1773 they established the London Bankers Clearing House to provide a central place where cheques could be exchanged between themselves. As time went by, they opened accounts with the Bank of England where they deposited their spare funds.

As the joint-stock banks grew in size and importance, the Bank of England began to develop as the central bank with which all the other banks held accounts. The circulation of private bank notes declined and Bank of England notes became legal tender. During the twentieth century, the Bank of England has ceased to take on business that would put it into competition with the other banks.

During the two world wars, the Bank of England took on the responsibility for raising the finance needed by the Government, and for devising and implementing measures to deal with the financial and economic consequences of the war effort. In the post-war period, it had the task of restoring the country's financial and economic position through its monetary policies.

In 1946, the bank was considered to be of such national importance that it was nationalised under the Bank of England Act. The act gave the bank wide powers to control and regulate the banking and financial system.

Under the Banking Act of 1979, all the banks were brought under the jurisdiction of the Bank of England, and this was further tightened by the Banking Act of 1987.

BANK STATEMENT

This is a record of transactions that have taken place on a bank current account. They can be issued on a monthly, bi-monthly or quarterly basis, depending on the amount of use the account is put to, and the needs of the customer. There is usually a delay of up to a week between a transaction taking place and its appearance on a bank statement, and for this reason, businesses need to produce a bank reconciliation statement to reconcile the bank statement with the amount showing in the business cash book.

BANKRUPTCY

A person may become bankrupt if a creditor brings proceedings against them for unpaid debts over £750. Once a bankruptcy order has been made by the courts, the affairs of the business are handed over to the Official Receiver who will then supervise the sale of the assets to cover the debts. In the case of a sole trader or a partnership, the individual's personal assets (house, cars, etc) may be sold to pay the debts of the business. Members of a partnership are 'jointly and severally liable' for the debts of the business. This means that creditors can pursue all or any one of the partners for the whole amount of the debt outstanding.

THE BANKRUPTCY ASSOCIATION

The association provides support and information to anyone facing bankruptcy. Their address is: The Bankruptcy Association, 4 Johnson Close, Abraham Heights, Lancaster LA1 5EU.

BARCLAY'S BANK

The direct history of Barclay's Bank can be traced back to a goldsmith-banker called John Freame whose father was a partner in the Three Anchors banking business in Lombard Street, London in the late seventeenth century. In 1728 John bought the adjacent Black Spread Eagle building and moved his office there. It later became the site of Barclays Head Office and the Spread Eagle became the internationally recognised symbol of Barclay's. James Barclay, John Freames's brother-in-law, was admitted to the partnership in 1736. Robert Barclay was a Quaker, and the strong Quaker connection remained a feature of Barclay's for generations and many of the amalgamations that took place during the eighteenth and nineteenth centuries were as a result of business interests complemented by a common faith. Quakers cultivated the virtues of simplicity, thrift and sobriety, and their temperament and attitudes fitted them well for the business of banking.

James Barclay's nephew, Silas Bevan, joined the company in 1767 and another relative by marriage, John Henton Tritton joined in 1782. Expansion started in 1863 when Barclay's amalgamated with Spooner, Attwood and Company. In 1888 the business grew still more by incorporating Ramson, Bouvierie and Company. Ransom's office in Pall Mall became the first Barclay's branch and the enlarged bank was called Barclay, Tritton, Ransom, Bouvierie and Company. Six years later, the bank acquired Hall, Bevan, West and Bevans of Brighton.

By 1896, many banks had united as joint-stock companies and Barclay's decided that this was the pattern for the future. It amalgamated with nineteen other independent banks from many parts of the country.

THE PRIVATE BANKS WHO JOINED TO FORM BARCLAY AND COMPANY LTD 1896

Jonathan Backhouse, Darlington

Sharples, Tuke, Lucas & Seebohm, Hitcham

Gurneys, Birkbeck, Barclay & Buxton, Norwich, and associated banks at Kings Lynn, Fakenham, Halesworth, Great Yarmouth, Wisbech, Ipswich and Colchester

Goslings & Sharpe, London

Sparrow, Tufnell & Co, Chelmsford and Braintree

Bassett, Son & Harris, Leighton Buzzard

Gibson, Tuke and Gibson, Saffron Walden

Fordham, Gibson & Co, Royston

J. Mortlock & Co, Cambridge

Veasey, Desborough, Bevan, Tillard & Co, Huntingdon

Molineaux, Whitfield & Co, Lewes

Woodhall, Hebden & Co, Scarborough

Barclay and Company wanted to retain the trading sign of the Black Spread Eagle, however, other ancient houses carried it in various forms, so the College of Arms ruled that the Eagle had to be 'differenced'. Other signs that were associated with Barclay-owned property in Lombard Street included the Bible, Three Crowns and the Three Kings. The devout Quaker partners refused to use the Bible as a symbol for trade, so the Eagle was given three kingly crowns, one on each wing, and one on the breast. The grant of arms was made officially in 1937.

Barclay's growth accelerated after the joint-stock amalgamation, with the company acquiring a succession of banks throughout the country. The management of Barclay's, however, remained very much a family affair, with descendants of the original directors still on the Board today.

In 1917, the company became Barclays Bank Ltd, and the merger with the London Provincial South Western Bank raised Barclays to the status of being one of the 'Big Four' English banks.

The hey-day of amalgamations came to an end in 1919 after the Colwyn Committee Report made it necessary for all bank mergers to be approved by the Bank of England and the Treasury. This stance was relaxed in 1967, which allowed the merger of Martins Bank in 1968. Martins ranked sixth largest in the country, and its 700 branches, predominantly in the north, subsequently became fully integrated into Barclays.

In the period between the two world wars, Barclays began to expand its interest internationally. In 1925, the Barclays Bank, (Dominion, Colonial and Overseas) was formed through a merger with the Colonial Bank, The Anglo Egyptian Bank and the National Bank of South Africa. It became Barclays Bank International in 1971.

As the former colonies emerged as independent nations after the Second World War, Barclays began to form partnerships with local organisations and governments. As new trading groups like the EEC were formed, Barclays responded with a major programme of acquisitions and development. Recent years have seen branches and subsidiaries opened in several European countries as well as South East Asia, the Pacific Basin, Latin America and North America. Barclays have cultivated close associations with the Bank of China and have now opened a Barclays office in Beijing.

Consequently, Barclays has a team of specialists that can help businesses with money management and the movement of money across the world. Barclays has also taken a major initiative with seminars designed to make exporters more aware of services available from other sources as well as from the bank.

During the 1960s and 1970s, in line with the other banks, Barclays concentrated on the development of its range of services. The bank was the first of British banks to install a computer for branch book-keeping in 1959, and pioneered the credit card revolution with the introduction of the Barclaycard in 1966.

Barclays remains committed to and proud of a tradition of local control and personal service. There are 35 local head offices in England and Wales run by directors who have considerable latitude to handle major financial deals without reference to central head office, however, the need for specialist advice to business has been recognised, and Barclays have over 200 specialist services, including the Business Advisory Service which was launched in 1973, to offer expert advice to smaller companies on budgeting, cash flow forecasting and other management accounting techniques.

Barclays believes that businessmen prefer to concentrate exclusively on their real job rather than on the paperwork, and this philosophy has influenced the various schemes they have developed for business including pension advisory schemes, factoring and taxation and insurance services.

THE BRITISH FRANCHISE ASSOCIATION

The British Franchise Association has some 80 full members and 30 or so registered associates. A full member has to have operated a successful pilot franchise scheme for at least one year and to have at least four franchisees operating at the end of a further two years. The Association produces a Franchise Information Pack for people who are interested in buying a franchise, which includes a list of members, associates and advisors, an audio tape and books.

Their address is: British Franchise Association, Francise Chambers, Thames View, Newtown Road, Henley-on-Thames, Oxon RG9 1HG.

BRITISH INSURANCE AND INVESTMENT BROKERS ASSOCIATION

The Association is the trade association for insurance and investment brokers. Their address is: BIIBA, 14 Bevis Marks, London EC3 7NT.

BUDGET

Businesses use budgets in many different ways, but the main purpose is always to control the financial operations of the business. Budgets can be used to:

- control expenditure in specific areas
- control and monitor costs
- streamline decision making
- plan expenditure
- monitor profit expectations
- identify problem areas
- prevent cash flow shortages.

BUILDING SOCIETIES

The earliest building societies were just what their name implies, societies whose members jointly saved up enough capital to construct homes for themselves. All members would contribute an equal sum of money at regular intervals to the fund and when enough had been accumulated, a plot of land would be bought and houses built on it. Houses were built singly and allocated to members by drawing lots. All members would continue to contribute to the fund until a house had been built for everyone, at which time the society would be wound up. These terminating societies were a self-help organisation owned and run by the members.

During the nineteenth century, societies began to be set up in which the members who contributed the funds to buy the houses were not necessarily the same people as the members who eventually lived in them. The depositing members had to be rewarded for the use of their money and this was done by paying them interest on it. The borrowing members were charged interest on the funds which were made available to them by the society. There was no reason why these permanent societies should ever be wound up while new depositors and borrowers could be found.

These permanent societies continued to grow and proliferate offering a fairly narrow range of facilities to just two classes of customer: personal savers and house buyers looking for a mortgage. They were given a formal legal nature with defined, if limited, objects by the Building Societies Act 1874. By 1900, there were 2,286 societies with £60 million assets between them. By 1940, this had reduced to just 952 societies, but their assets had grown to £756 million. In the 35 years to 1980 the societies had total dominance of housing finance, and their loan and other assets leapt to £54 billion. The societies largely had the home loans market to themselves as the banks were effectively barred from entering the field by the lending curbs imposed by the Government which helped influence and control the economy. Foreign financial groups were also excluded from the market by exchange controls.

An implicit condition of this protected market was that societies would operate a 'cartel' of interest rates, endeavouring to keep the rates as low as possible. Governments closely watched these rates and on one occasion paid a subsidy to prevent them from rising. To fund their lending, the societies relied on the thrift of individuals, to whom they appealed with such effect that by 1980 they had attracted nearly half the nation's personal short-term savings. Unlike banks, they could not shop for cash in the cheaper City money markets. Competition between societies was not on the price of loans, but on the quality of the service and the availability of branches, whose numbers in the High Street trebled to 6,163 in the eleven years to 1981.

Despite the societies' success, there was a chronic mortgage shortage during the 1970s and early 1980s. The steadily increasing proportion of owner-occupation and tax breaks fuelling the underlying demand for house buying, the demand for home loans could not be met and rationing was often needed.

With the election of the Conservative Government in 1979, there was a gradual shift to deregulation and less shutting off of sectors from each other. Exchange controls on payments to and from abroad were scrapped and in mid-1980 domestic loan controls were removed from the big banks.

Thus freed to compete in the safe and potentially lucrative mortgage market, the banks moved in strength and by 1981 had captured a 26 per cent share of new lending. With their protected market gone, the societies had to shop more extensively in the money markets, and pressure soon built for greater freedom to seek funds elsewhere. Societies felt frustrated by their exclusion from wholesale money markets so it became a major objective of the building societies to persuade the Government to give them a more flexible structure from which to compete.

In mid-1981 the Building Societies Association established a group to review the societies' constitution, powers and the law governing them. The report was published in 1983 and it recommended that while retaining their basic character, building societies should be allowed to undertake a wider range of functions, and in particular should be allowed to branch out into connected services such as estate agency and conveyancing, supply limited personal and other additional loans, and provide certain retail banking facilities including current cheque accounts and credit cards.

A Green Paper outlining the Government's proposals to reform the societies was issued in July 1984, and the Act, which gave the societies most of what they wanted, became law in 1986, and inspired a revolution in the structure and services provided by the societies. Many of the societies began to introduce cheque accounts and credit cards, and a number bought or established chains of estate agents. With access to the City money markets, they were able to compete directly with the banks, not only on mortgages, but also in the field of retail banking, insurance and other private banking services. Their longer opening hours, computerised services and branch and agency network made them ideally placed to take full advantage of the market. Some of the smaller societies, however, remained firmly where they were. Without the resources of the national societies, they decided to concentrate on highly competitive interest rates for savers and an increased range of investment opportunities, rather than diversify into retail banking and associated business.

BUSINESS PLAN

The two main purposes of a business plan are to provide information to prospective investors/lenders to the business and to provide a means of control once the business is operational.

A good business plan should contain:

- a summary of the business potential, with forecast profit figures
- a summary of past performance of the business or, if it is a new business starting up, a summary of the skills and knowledge of the person(s) embarking on the new venture
- the employment and business experience of the people working with you

- a description of the product or service being offered by the business
- market research information
- a marketing plan
- a promotion plan
- operational details, such as location, suppliers, manufacturing facilities and equipment needed
- financial analysis, which should include forecasted cash flow and profit and loss figures, and a break-even analysis
- the prospects for the business.

C

CAPITAL

Capital is the money used to start a business, plus accumulated profit over successive years. Any losses are deducted from the capital. In accounting terms,

$$Capital = assets - liabilities$$

CASH

Cash is the amount of money in a business, but should not be confused with profit. It is possible for a business to be 'cash-rich' at a certain moment in time while still making a loss. Similarly, a business with good on-paper profits can have a cash flow deficit, maybe because a large client has failed to pay up!

CASH FLOW FORECAST

This is a method of predicting and reviewing the cash flow of a business, with the aim of preventing unscheduled cash flow deficits. It enables the business to take preventative action if a deficit is predicted and to avoid the additional expense and possible danger to the business of not having sufficient cash to meet its debts.

CHARGE CARDS

Charge cards are similar to credit cards in that it is a non-cash method of paying for goods. Unlike credit cards, however, they do not normally have a credit limit, and it is expected that the outstanding balance is settled at the end of each month. Diners Club and American Express are examples of this type of card.

CHARTERED ASSOCIATION OF CERTIFIED ACCOUNTANTS

Accountants who qualify as members of this association have ACCA or FCCA after their names. Membership is dependent on accountants completing a required course of training and complying with the Code of Practice set out by the association. The Association is recognised by the Department of Trade as an authorised Auditing body. Their address is: The Chartered Association of Certified Accountants, 29 Lincoln's Inn Fields, London WC2A 3EE.

COMPANIES REGISTRATION OFFICE

The companies registration office hold the records of all companies registered in the UK. It has offices in Cardiff, Edinburgh and Belfast.

CONTRACT HIRE

This is a method of obtaining use of motor vehicles as an alternative to hire purchase and leasing. It involves the long-term hire of vehicles, where servicing and repairs are included in the contract.

CORPORATION OF INDEPENDENT FINANCIAL ADVISORS

This is the trade association for independent financial advisors. They can provide a list of members on request.

CREDIT

The term 'credit' is used in two ways in business. In accounting terms, it is used to describe an entry on the right hand side of a ledger account, to indicate either the increase in a liability, the decrease of an asset or an item of revenue.

In general terms, the word credit is used to describe a means of deferring payment for goods.

CREDIT CARD

A credit card is a means of deferring payment for goods and services. The holder of the card receives a statement at the end of each month showing the purchases that have been made and the amount outstanding on the account. Unlike a charge card (see above) it is not necessary to pay the full amount at the end of each month. Interest is charged on the outstanding unpaid balance. Credit cards are accepted worldwide, and can also be used to obtain local currency from ATMs. Cash can also be withdrawn in the UK. An additional charge is made for this facility.

CREDIT CONTROL

Credit control is essential to any business that buys or sells goods on credit. It ensures that money is received from debtors on time and reduces the likelihood of unexpected cash flow deficits. It also ensures that customers do not exceed the limits of credit set and thus increase the risk of unrecoverable debts. A good credit control system will also monitor the amount of credit taken by the business and ensure that the business debts are paid on time, avoiding the possibility of action being taken by a creditor through the courts.

D

DEBT

This is money owed by a business. Failure to pay the debts of a business can lead to bankruptcy of a sole trader or a partnership, or the compulsory winding up of a limited company.

DEBTORS (TRADE)

Trade debtors are customers who have bought goods on credit from the business.

DEPRECIATION

This is an allowance made in the accounts of a business which takes into account the falling value of a fixed asset due to wear and tear, obsolescence or other factors which will reduce its value over time. The allowance is made to ensure that the assets of the business are not over-valued.

There are two methods of calculating depreciation, the straight line method, where a fixed amount is deducted from the value of the asset each year, and the reducing balance method which deducts a fixed percentage from the written down value of the asset. The reducing balance method is generally favoured by the Inland Revenue.

DIRECTORS

Directors are the executive (policy and decision making) management of a limited company. They may or may not be shareholders of the company. The Board of Directors are responsible for the overall management of the company, and may be elected or removed by the shareholders, to whom they are ultimately accountable.

DISCOUNT

There are generally two types of discount that can be given or received, a discount for the purchase of large quantities, or for placing a regular order, and discount given for prompt payment of an account. Quantity discount sometimes has to be negotiated with a supplier, and sometimes it is built into the standard price list. Discount for prompt payment is normally used by business to encourage payments to be on time. However, it requires a competent level of credit control to ensure that only customers who are entitled to the discount actually receive it, as there is a tendency for debtors to deduct the discount on payment whether they are entitled to it or not!

DIVIDENDS

Dividends are the share of the profits that is paid to shareholders, and is usually quoted as an amount for each share held. Dividends are usually 'declared' at the Annual General Meeting when the accounts for the preceding year are presented.

Many larger companies will declare an interim dividend at the end of each half year which will then be adjusted when the accounts are presented at the end of the financial year.

E

ENTERPRISE AGENCIES

Enterprise agencies are a national network of independent, non-profit making organisations set up to help and advise small businesses in their area. They vary considerably in size across the country, and in the way in which they are funded. They are able to offer information and advice, training courses, advice on the availability of premises and workshop units, and advice on grants and loans that are available in a particular area.

ESTATE AGENTS

In addition to providing a market for domestic housing, many estate agents have a commercial section which brings together people with commercial premises to rent or for sale with those who are looking for premises. They are also able to offer help and advice should a structural survey be required when buying the freehold or a lease on premises, assist with the negotiation with landlords or vendors, and advice on whether planning permission or a change of use is required from the local authority. In some circumstances they can also provide information and advice on funding.

EUROPEAN INFORMATION CENTRE NETWORK

There are 25 European Information Centres which have been set up by the European Commission to help small and medium sized companies take advantage of the single European market.

F

FACTORING

Factoring is a process by which a business sells its debts to a factor in return for cash. The service offered by a factor is wide and the complete service could involve the factor in taking over the operation of the whole of a business's sales ledger. The separate components of factoring, i.e. record keeping, cash collection, invoice discounting (see below) and credit insurance are available individually from a number of different organisations. Generally, factoring is not available to businesses with a turnover of less than £100,000 per annum, and the factor will investigate the trading record, bad debt history credit rating procedures and customers of the business before deciding to offer a factoring service. A business can expect to receive somewhere in the region of 80 per cent of the invoice value of its debts.

Factoring can be very useful to some businesses but it can prove expensive. The business is likely to have to enter into an agreement for not less than a year.

FIMBRA

FIMBRA is the regulatory authority for independent intermediaries who give advice on such matters as pensions, investments, and life assurance. Part of the work of FIMBRA will be taken over by the PIA.

FINANCE HOUSES

Finance houses developed in the second half of the nineteenth century, largely to finance the development of the coal industry. Their primary purpose was to finance railway wagons for the transport of coal, and the word 'Wagon' still features in the names of some companies operating today. With the advent of the motor car, the companies moved into the field of financing vehicles, and later into consumer goods such as furniture, carpets and electrical goods. All of the clearing banks now have an interest in finance houses — such as the National Westminster Bank's acquisition of Lombard North Central — and market their services through their branch network. Some of those finance houses that have remained independent have developed the idea of the 'money shop' located in High Street shopping centres, with hours linked to shopping hours rather than banking hours.

Finance houses obtain their funds by borrowing from banks and other financial institutions, and by accepting deposits from industrial and commercial companies, and private individuals.

FIRE INSURANCE

This type of insurance protects a business from destruction or damage to building and their contents from fire. Some policies can also insure the business against the loss of income that may result from a fire in their premises. This type of insurance is often part of a 'package' which will also provide protection from other risks such as lightning, explosion, aircraft, storm damage, flood, riot and malicious damage.

FORECASTING

Forecasts are at the heart of any business. They are the basis on which a business raises money, negotiates premises and orders raw materials — just a few of the many decisions that a business has to make on a day-to-day basis which have to be based on a forecast of some sort. It is important to realise, however, that the phrase 'garbage in, garbage out' is as applicable to forecasting as it is to computers, so forecasts have to be made on realistic assumptions about the business's future, and on realistic data produced by the record-keeping systems.

There are three main forecasts on which a business needs to make realistic decisions — a cash flow forecast, predicted profit and loss statements, and projected balance sheets. All forecasts are guesswork, but they must be made as error free as possible to enable the business to function at its best, and avoid any nasty surprises in the future.

FOREIGN BANKS

There are now over 500 different foreign banks operating in Britain, mostly situated in London, although some are beginning to establish branch networks in major cities outside London. Banks from other countries have had a presence in the UK since the nineteenth century, as London established itself as the principal international banking centre. While some have only a representative office which does not transact normal banking business, many have established branches, providing a full range of banking services.

Generally, foreign banks wish to be represented in Britain:

- to develop trade between Britain and the overseas country
- to provide financial services for businessmen from overseas visiting Britain
- to provide banking services to immigrants and foreign nationals living and working in Britain
- to act as international bankers on behalf of businesses overseas:

Some of the foreign banks have established branch networks and are competing directly with the clearing banks by offering services aimed at the personal customer, particularly in areas where people from their own countries have settled.

The development of North Sea oil and the increasing international investment that has been taking place, particularly between Britain and the USA, has been the main reason for the foreign banks setting up in the UK. The American banks have been in the forefront of this development, and there are now some 60 American banks operating in the UK, with more American banks in London than there are in New York.

FRANCHISING

Buying into a franchise is a popular and frequently successful method of going into business for the first time. When someone buys a franchise (becomes a franchisee) they are buying a complete business system or way of trading from the franchisor (seller of the franchise). A well set up franchise reduces the risks involved with setting up a new business, as the franchisee is buying a tried and tested product and method of doing business. It can be expensive, though, particularly for a nationally known franchise name, but this can be offset by the continuing training, advice and promotion provided by the franchisor.

G

GOING CONCERN

This phrase is used to describe a trading business. In accounting terms, the assumption when preparing final accounts is that the business will continue to trade.

GOODWILL

Goodwill is the value of a business above and beyond the value of the assets. It is normally only calculated when the business is sold, and will not appear on the balance sheet. The valuation of goodwill will include such things as the value of client lists, the experience of employees and the reputation of the business.

GRANTS

There are a wide variety of grants, allowances and cheap loans made to new businesses by Government, local authority and charities, particularly if the business is located in an Urban Programme area or an Assisted Area. Government grants are also available to businesses which are developing innovative or technological advances which can be used to develop the product.

GUARANTEES (FOR LOANS)

In some circumstances, for example where a business has got into difficulties, a lender may only provide additional finance if someone is prepared to stand as guarantor for the additional funding. In the case of a limited company, the directors may be asked to guarantee the loan personally. In the case of a sole trader or a partnership, the lender may ask that a third party stands as guarantor for the loan, that is, they agree to take on the responsibility for the loan if the sole trader or partner is unable to repay the debt.

H

HEALTH INSURANCE

Permanent health insurance provides an income if someone is too ill to work or is permanently disabled by an illness. Some policies provide for accident insurance, and some provide both accident and sickness cover. This type of insurance is useful for anyone who maybe has family and financial responsibilities which are dependent on their regular income. People in employment are usually covered by both a company sickness scheme as well as the State National Insurance sickness benefit, and therefore may consider permanent health insurance an 'optional extra'. Someone who is self-employed, however, will probably find this type of insurance essential to protect both their families and their business should they be disabled by an accident or a serious illness.

HIRE PURCHASE

Hire purchase is a means of financing the purchase of assets for a business, or items for personal use. Ownership of the goods passes to the purchaser when the final payment on the agreement is made. For businesses, the asset will appear on the balance sheet from the time the business begins to use it, with the amount owing showing as a liability. Capital allowances are claimable on the goods from the time the business begins to use it. Payments of interest (but not the repayment of the capital) are allowable against tax.

I

INCORPORATED SOCIETY OF VALUERS AND AUCTIONEERS

Members of the society will give advice on valuation of and negotiation for property. A list of members can be obtained from the Incorporated Society of Valuers and Auctioneers, 3 Cadogan Gate, London SW1X 0AP.

INDEPENDENT INTERMEDIARY

Independent intermediaries are not registered brokers but are selling general insurance such as motor or building insurance. Intermediaries who give information and advice about personal financial matters such as pensions and investment-type life insurance such as endowment policies, must be registered with a regulatory body such as FIMBRA. Registration does not mean that an intermediary will do a great deal of research work on the client's behalf, or necessarily obtain the best deal. While in theory an independent intermediary can deal with a wide range of insurance products, not all will be able or willing to offer all that is on the market. It is therefore worth approaching more than one source of insurance or financial advice. Independent intermediaries are not obliged to have professional indemnity insurance (though many have, for their own protection) or to contribute to a compensation fund. They should, however, comply with the Code of Practice established by the Association of British Insurers.

INFLATION

Inflation is the word used to describe a rise in prices as reflected in changes in the Retail Price Index. Figures are published monthly by the Central Statistical Office, and compare prices this month with the same month last year (annual inflation rate) or this month with last month (month-on month rate).

INSOLVENCY

A company becomes insolvent when it is unable to pay its debts. Insolvency will require the winding up of the company and sale of its assets to repay the debts. This can be done voluntarily with the agreement of 75 per cent of the members of the company, or may be forced by a creditor or bank applying to the court for compulsory winding up of the company under the Insolvency Act 1986.

INSTITUTE OF CHARTERED ACCOUNTANTS

The institute is one of the recognised bodies of accountants who have ACA or FCA after their names. Members of the Institute of Chartered Accountants of Scotland have CA after their names. The head office addresses are: Institute of Chartered Accountants in England and Wales, PO Box 433, Chartered Accountants Hall, Moorgate Place, London, EC2P 2BJ; Institute of Chartered Accountants of Scotland, 27 Queen Street, Edinburgh EH2 1LA.

INSTITUTE OF MANAGEMENT CONSULTANTS

Members of the institute provide business and management consultancy services to a wide range of businesses. Their head office address is: Institute of Management Consultants, 5th Floor, 32-33 Hatton Garden, London EC1N 8DL.

INSURANCE COMPANIES

The major function of insurance companies is to pool the resources of many people to provide for unforeseen contingencies, or to provide financial assistance in the event of death. The money received in premiums is invested in a wide range of British Government and company securities, which provides a pool of funds from which claims may be met. Their experience in the field of investment makes them ideal intermediaries to act as managers for the investment of pension fund contributions.

The business of an insurance company is usually split into two sections, long-term insurance, which is life assurance and long-term sickness assurance, and general insurance, which deals with all the other areas, such as motor, property, personal and accident insurance.

The insurance industry is a highly complex and specialised business, with more than 20 major British companies offering a wide range of services to business and personal customers. Eagle Star, for example, offer over 100 different 'main line' highly specialised policies to large business customers, while Commercial Union offers a wide range of 'safety net' packages, which will include a combination of cover for building, contents and specialised risks for smaller businesses, tailor-made for the different trading sectors, e.g. hoteliers, retailers, motor traders, etc.

INTEREST

Interest is the cost of money. It is the amount that is charged for lending money to an individual or an institution. If you deposit money in a bank or building society, you are effectively lending them the money, which they in turn either invest in another institution, or lend to other borrowers. The interest rate paid on deposits will therefore reflect the length of time the money is deposited, and the rate will rise the longer the money is committed for. The rate of interest can be expressed in two ways, as a flat rate, or more usually, as an Annual Percentage Rate (APR). APR allows an investor or borrower to compare rates of interest offered by lenders and investments over different time scales and different terms and conditions. For example, it is possible to compare the rate charged on a credit card, where interest is charged on a monthly basis, with that charged on a personal loan, where the interest may be calculated differently.

K

KEYMAN INSURANCE

This type of insurance can give protection to a business that is dependent on a few key people. It is possible to provide the business with a lump sum payment should one of these key people die while working for the business. In order to take out this type of cover, a business must be able to prove that the person's death will cost the business money.

L

LAWYERS FOR YOUR BUSINESS SCHEME

This scheme provides a free initial consultation for those running young or growing businesses, plus a clear indication of what further advice might cost. Further information about the scheme can be obtained from The Law Society, 50-52 Chancery Lane, London WC2A 1SX.

LEASING

Leasing is a means of renting the assets that a business needs for its operations. Leasing is most commonly used for premises, plant, machinery and motor vehicles, but can be applied to almost any fixed asset a business needs. The business does not own the items involved, so they do not appear on the balance sheet. Leasing payments are allowable against tax, but capital allowances are not available for leased items. Leasing offers an additional degree of flexibility to a business. Leasing agreements often (but not always) include some form of servicing contract, and can be useful when technology is advancing rapidly and continual updating of equipment is desirable to keep up with competition, for example in the area of computers, photocopiers and computer controlled machinery. Leasing also provides an alternative form of finance for assets.

LEGAL EXPENSES INSURANCE

This would provide insurance against the expenses involved in a contractual or employment dispute, or certain other legal procedures.

LIABILITIES

These are essentially what the business owes to third parties, and includes such things as creditors, loans and capital. Capital is a liability because ultimately it is owed back to the owner(s) of a business.

LIQUIDATOR

A liquidator will take responsibility for the winding up of a business if the business becomes insolvent. The liquidator may be appointed by the creditors or the Official Receiver, and will ensure that the assets of the business are used to pay off the creditors.

LLOYDS BANK

In June 1765 the firm of Taylors & Lloyds opened for business at Dale End in Birmingham. Like most private bankers of the eighteenth century, the partners had made their money in other fields. John Taylor, a Unitarian, was a maker of buttons and japanned goods, while Sampson Lloyd, a Quaker, was an ironmaster. Unlike some other bankers, however, they did not continue their original business ventures alongside their new profession.

For almost 100 years the private bank had only one Birmingham office and no branches. The Lloyds soon became the more active family and the association of the Taylors ended in 1852. During the difficult years of the eighteenth and early nineteenth century when many private banks failed, the partnership was never in difficulties or even seriously tested, but eventually it became necessary to broaden the capital base of the bank by changing its status to a joint-stock company. For some years they had been in competition with large and integrated banking companies, many of which had limited liability and were better organised to meet the Victorian industrial boom.

Following the formation of Lloyds Banking Company there was an explosion of growth. Branches were opened in Oldbury, Tamworth Halesowen and elsewhere, while other outlets were acquired in Staffordshire and Warwickshire by the first of a long series of mergers with smaller banks, and by the mid 1880s Lloyds had established itself as a powerful banking force in the Midlands.

As early as 1771 the sons of the original Birmingham partners, aided by two associates, had opened a bank in Lombard Street, London, and in 1884 this business was absorbed into the mainstream bank.

The Lombard Street address is of particular interest because it brought about the connection of Lloyds Bank with the black horse. The bank's earlier symbol had been the beehive, but adopted the black horse which had a direct descent from a goldsmith called Humphrey Stokes or Stocks, who was known to keen 'running cashes', roughly equivalent of current accounts, in the seventeenth century. The black horse was considered to be representative of the growing London interests, and was appearing generally on stationery and cheques when the bank's name changed to Lloyds Bank Ltd in the 1890s.

After 1884 mergers gathered even greater pace and banks throughout the country were added. The two biggest mergers were at either end of the Great War: The Wilts & Dorset Bank, with around 100 offices, was acquired in 1914 and the Capital and Counties Bank, with 473, in 1918. The take-overs continued and included Fox, Fowler & Co of Wellington Somerset, the last private firm to issue its own bank notes. By 1923 there had been some 50 direct take-overs and the business of nearly three times that number of banks had descended to Lloyds Bank by virtue of earlier take-overs made by some of its constituent banks.

From the early 1920s until mid 1960s Lloyds Bank operated in the UK as one of the 'Big Five'. However the bank had already begun to show an interest in the international scene which was later to play an important part in its development. In 1911 the business of Armstrong and Co, based in Paris and Le Havre, was acquired. From 1917, this company was run jointly as the Lloyds and National Provincial Foreign Bank, but Lloyds Bank bought full ownership in 1955. The bank then became Lloyds Bank (Foreign), later Lloyds Bank Europe.

The interest in banking in South America began in 1918 when Lloyds Bank acquired the London & River Plate Bank. This bank was merged in 1923 with the London & Brazil Bank to form the Bank of London and South America (BOLSA), in which Lloyds Bank retained a significant interest,. BOLSA grew subsequently to become the principal British commercial banking presence in Latin America.

The challenges of the 1980s confronted Lloyds as it did the other banks, and for Lloyds the answer was seen to lie in investing only in activities that earned a return on capital higher than the cost of capital. This led to the bank needing to divest itself of business representing some 20 per cent of shareholders funds and to reinvest the proceeds in activities having more profit potential. The latter included insurance, mortgage lending and the estate agency business in the UK, and private banking in Germany through the purchase of the business of Schroder, Munchmeyerm, Hengst & Co.

1986 saw the merger of Lloyds Bank International into Lloyds Bank, and the creation of Lloyds Merchant Bank, and in 1988 the bank merged five of its businesses with Abbey Life insurance company to create Lloyds Abbey Life, a new insurance-led group controlled by the Bank, marketing life assurance, unit trusts, insurance broking, estate agency and the finance house services of Lloyds Bowmaker. This was a significant step by the bank, designed to build its personal customer base and maintain profitability through an extended range of financial services.

LLOYD'S OF LONDON

Lloyd's of London is the world's leading insurance market transacting business worth billions of pounds each year. It is not an insurance company (and has no connection with Lloyd's Bank) and does not itself accept insurance risks. It acts as a market, bringing together those who require insurance with syndicates of individuals and corporate members who are willing to underwrite that risk in return for a premium.

Syndicates range in size from a hundred or so up to several thousand members. Every individual member (known as Names) of Lloyd's, currently around 18,000, has proved wealth of at least £250,000 and trades individually with unlimited liability. Corporate members, who were first allowed to participate in the market in 1994, require a minimum capitalisation of £1.5 million.

Syndicates are administered by managing agents who are responsible for employing the underwriter and his staff and ensuring that business is conducted within the requirements of bylaws and regulations laid down under Lloyd's Act. Members' agents introduce new members to the market, provide advice and administer a number of their Lloyd's affairs other than underwriting.

When an individual or company wishes to buy insurance, they approach one of the 220 registered Lloyd's brokers who will discuss the risk and advise the client how best to package the cover. The broker will then go to an underwriter who specialises in whichever class of business he wishes to place and describes the risk and explains the client's insurance requirements. If the underwriter is satisfied that the risk is viable, he will quote a 'rate' to the broker, which is usually expressed as a percentage of the risk's total value, and after some negotiation, a premium is agreed. Sometimes an underwriter will agree to cover the whole of the risk, sometimes, if the risk is a particularly large one, only part, in which case, the broker will then have to approach other underwriters until the whole of the risk is covered. If the underwriter is not satisfied that the risk represents good business for his syndicate, then he will turn it down, and the broker must then seek another underwriter with whom to negotiate the terms and conditions of the cover required.

In the event of a claim, each syndicate is liable for the proportion of the risk for which the underwriter has signed. Most marine, non-marine and aviation claims are processed on behalf of underwriters by Lloyd's Claims Office, a centralised service administered by the Corporation of Lloyd's. Claims are paid to the client through the broker.

An underwriter's day at Lloyd's

To describe how the London market works and to provide insight into some aspects of the Lloyd's competitive advantages, we developed a picture of what takes place in an underwriter's day.

For one large marine syndicate that we visited, the underwriter's day begins at 8.00 am with a meeting of all the underwriters for that syndicate, held at the offices of the underwriting agency. All underwriters at Lloyd's are nominally employed by a syndicate, but they are supported by the underwriting agency that hired and placed them with the syndicate that it is contracted to manage.

The meeting is run by the senior underwriter for the syndicate, who is designated as the 'active underwriter'. He is personally responsible to Lloyd's and to the Names on the syndicate for the conduct of the syndicate's underwriters. Also at the meeting are the deputy underwriter and six other underwriters, who are assigned to various classes of marine risk, including hull, cargo, war risk and marine liability. Even the active underwriter and his deputy have their areas of special expertise. In the meeting, each underwriter reviews two books that together contain a summary of each risk written the preceding day. The active underwriter comments on some of the risks. The subsequent discussion centres on desirable and undesirable features of the risks written and how to make them more attractive to the underwriter by, for example, adding particular terms and conditions. The meeting lasts about two hours.

The underwriters then move to their individual offices for about an hour of reviewing the correctness and completeness of the working of policies that have been issued from the 'slips' on which they committed the syndicate for a particular set of terms and conditions.

As 11.00 am approaches, the underwriters walk to Lloyd's to receive visits at the syndicate's box by brokers seeking to introduce new business, negotiate terms on cases already introduced, or close on a risk once additional information or other underwriters' approval has been obtained. With time out for lunch, the underwriter spends about five hours at the box. On the day of our visit, he received visits from some 25 brokers. Of those, five were for new business: one straightforward risk (a yacht) was accepted, three were declined as not consistent with the type of risk written by the syndicate, and the underwriter asked for more information for the fifth one.

All the other visits were follow-ups of risks previously introduced. Some conversations were very short — one took less than a minute to agree on an endorsement that the underwriter had seen many times before. Exceptionally, a visit with one of the senior underwriters by a broker hoping to obtain a 'lead' on a complex risk can take up to two hours.

At the box with underwriters are a two-person claims team and a support staff of four clerks. The clerks enter the data in the computer and produce reports for the underwriters. Any questions about classification of risk or interpretation of hand writing are dealt with on the spot, thus avoiding subsequent time-consuming messages among departments. Once entered in the computers, the data is accessible to all underwriters via the terminals at the box.

Lunch is usually taken with clients. Lloyd's underwriters generally will meet with senior officials of the businesses they underwrite, and lunch or dinner is the best time to do this. Our underwriter had three such lunches scheduled that week. The active underwriter usually has all five lunches committed, as well as some dinners.

At the end of the day at Lloyd's (about 5.30 pm) the underwriter returns to the offices for about an hour to review statistical reports on new business, claims, etc. At the office are other support staff dedicated to the syndicate — in this case, five claims technicians and four reinsurance specialists. (This syndicate's staff numbers are relatively large: it is a 'lead' syndicate, and thus, it shoulders some additional administrative and technical tasks on behalf of the 'following' underwriters.) Other support staff members are shared with other syndicates in the agency: computer, finance and secretarial support.

Source: Salomon Brothers — Lloyd's and the London Insurance market

LLOYD'S NAMES

In 1990, Lloyd's of London announced its largest losses (in absolute terms) in its 300 year history, some £2.9 billion, bringing many of its individual syndicate members, who operate with unlimited liability, close to bankruptcy. This loss represented 14.5 per cent of gross written premiums, with marine insurance representing more than half the total underwriting loss.

A series of natural and industrial disasters occurred including the explosion on the Piper Alpha oil rig, the San Francisco earthquake disaster and freak storms in the USA, southern England, the Netherlands and West Germany. There were also less dramatic, but equally costly increased claims in the fields of marine and motor insurance. These events combined to push many syndicates to the point of insolvency, and threatened Lloyd's proud boast to have never failed to pay on a valid claim. Many syndicates withdrew from the market, were taken over, or simply folded resulting in spiralling premium rates and a great deal of panic.

Many of the Names resorted to litigation over their losses. More than 800 names, including many well-known industrialists, MPs and sports and television personalities, instituted legal proceedings against RHM Outhwaite underwriting agency and 81 firms of members agents, claiming that Mr Outhwaite was negligent in insuring 40 other insurers against their liabilities relating to asbestos and pollution. Lloyd's in turn, replied with threats of court action for recovery of unpaid debts, and at one point, the Government itself was threatened, as a number of MPs faced bankruptcy which would disbar them from being Members of Parliament, and could therefore reduce the Government's majority to a point where it could no longer govern effectively.

The claims and counter-claims rumble on even now, although the emphasis during the last year or so has been on reaching a settlement, rather than pursuing claims to the bitter end. However, Lloyd's could not escape the fact that there were deep seated problems with the 300 year old institution, and radical reforms were necessary to restore confidence and stability in the worlds biggest insurance market. The election of a new Chairman in 1990 ushered in a period of re-structuring and reform, such as the introduction of personal lines when some motor syndicates began to offer their products direct to the public for the first time, and the link-up with Sun Alliance in a bid to secure new business elsewhere in Europe. Lloyd's Task Force was set up to conduct a year long investigation and a corporate plan entitled 'Planning for profit: a business plan for Lloyd's of London' was implemented in April 1993 as a direct result of their findings. The aim of the plan was to raise fresh capital from new types of investors and to find ways of protecting investors from further deteriorations in results on very old business.

Lloyd's intends to reinsure all the Names' liabilities still outstanding on policies written prior to 1986 into a new re-insurance company known as Newco, by the end of 1996. Newco will be capitalised by a transfer from Lloyd's central fund and from the surplus generated by discounting loss reserves. Corporate investors were introduced for the first time in June

1994, and Names will be allowed to structure as limited liability companies for underwriting. A wide programme to reduce expenses is being introduced including extending the use of information technology and a reduction in staffing.

Lloyd's of London remains one of the most mysterious and tradition-bound institutions in Britain, but its survival has major implications for the insurance industry and the economy as a whole. With litigation due to continue to rumble through the courts for some years to come, only time will tell if the changes already implemented and the proposals due to be introduced during the next few years will succeed in breaking through the attitudes and practice established over the last 300 years and produce an institution able to deal with the demands of the 21st century.

M

MERCHANT BANKS

There are today, some 100 institutions in the UK which call themselves merchant banks. They are financial institutions which provide specialist services to business including corporate finance, portfolio management, and other banking services. Many began business in the late eighteenth and early nineteenth centuries, and their early development was similar to that of the clearing banks, except that the merchant founders traded overseas rather than in Britain. As world trade expanded in the nineteenth century, these merchants grew in reputation and found themselves being asked to accept bills of exchange by lesser-known traders. The 'bill on London' became the main instrument of payment for all goods traded internationally, and became the preferred method of payment.

With the development of overseas trade, the merchants became known not only as bankers, but also as consultants by traders, private customers overseas, and local and central government. They would be asked for advice on raising loans by foreign governments and, as a result, they made a considerable contribution to making London the major world centre for the issue of foreign government bonds.

The two world wars and the consequent shrinkage of world trade hit the merchant banks. Exchange controls restricted the movement of money around the world and the banks were forced to expand their services into other areas. When world trade eased in the 1960s, they experienced heavy competition from the other banks, so they began to concentrate their energies in the field of corporate finance, and in particular their role in share issues and obtaining stock exchange quotations for shares.

While the range of services provided by merchant banks is variable from institution to institution, the following are examples of the type of services offered:

- portfolio management — the management of investments on behalf of pension funds, investment trusts, unit trusts and individuals.
- banking services — current, deposit and fixed-term deposit accounts, mainly for company customers.
- factoring
- hire purchase and leasing.

The merchant banks have also become involved with the international money or eurocurrency markets, and the international capital, or eurobond market. They often act for the UK and foreign companies and state enterprises to assist in the raising of medium and long-term finance.

During the last 20 years, all of the 'Big Four' clearing banks have bought interests in merchant banks, or have set up one of their own, for example, the one third share in Montague Trust, owners of Samuel Montague & Co, purchased by Midland Bank, and many of the corporate services of the clearing banks are offered through their merchant banking subsidiary.

MIDLAND BANK

Midland Bank first opened for business in Union Street, Birmingham on Monday, 22 August 1836. The bank was the inspiration of its first manager, Charles Geach, a 28 year old Cornishman who had previously been employed by the Bank of England at its Birmingham branch. Geach had strong support from leading Birmingham merchants and manufacturers who quickly provided the core of the capital and business for the new bank. From its foundation, Midland was a joint-stock bank, which retained

Geach's close relationships with the Bank of England by maintaining an account there and issuing its bank notes.

Midland's close relationships with the Bank of England and with major industrial and commercial interests in the region contributed much to its success and its ability to survive the successive banking crises of the mid 1800s. Midland made its first experiments in branch banking by purchasing the Stourbridge Old Bank in 1851 and Nicols Baker and Crane at Bewdley in 1862. By the mid 1870s, Midland had become the second largest of the Birmingham banks and twentieth in terms of capital in England and Wales. Limited liability was adopted in 1880. The industrial and financial depression of 1878-79 persuaded Midland to broaden its customer base, and from the late 1870s the bank began a programme of opening new branches in the region.

During the next decade, Midland embarked on a succession of take-overs which raised the total number of branches from three to 45 by 1890. It then decided to expand outside the Midlands with the purchase of the Central Bank of London in 1891 and the City Bank in 1898, which promoted Midland to become one of the four largest banks in the United Kingdom. A series of take-overs during the next two decades made Midland the largest bank in the world by 1918.

The key figure in this remarkable advance was Edward Holden, joint general manager from 1891-97, managing director from 1898-1908, and finally chairman and managing director from 1908 until his death in 1919.

In addition to its acquisition policy, Midland also pursued a long-term plan of opening new branches in areas where it was poorly represented, particularly in the south west, East Anglia. By 1919 Midland had over 1,400 branches in England and Wales.

The period of expansion at home was accompanied by an expansion of its interests abroad. In 1905, Midland was the first of the British commercial banks to establish a department for foreign exchange.

The amalgamations continued throughout the 1920s and 1930s, until British banking was dominated by the 'Big Five' clearing banks. These banks then entered an agreement with the government that they would not attempt any further amalgamations without Treasury approval. Midland continued its policy of opening new branches, especially in fast growing metropolitan and suburban areas, with over 2,100 branches in operation by 1939.

After the destruction of the Second World War and the period of austerity that followed, the 1960s saw a period of increased competition in British banking. Midland concentrated on reorganising its branch network and innovation in the range of banking services it offered. Gift cheques, personal current accounts, special loans for farmers, term loans for small businesses and cheque guarantee cards were all introduced during this period. The first cash dispensers appeared in 1968 and Access credit cards in 1972.

During the same period, Midland began to diversify into business areas outside traditional banking. The first of these initiatives was the acquisition of Forward Trust, the instalment finance company, which gave Midland access to the expanding hire purchase market. Midland invested heavily in Forward Trust during the 1960s, using its existing branch network to market the instalment finance and leasing packages. The member companies of Forward Trust Group also included Griffin Factors, the factoring company which became a wholly-owned subsidiary in 1974, and Concord Leasing (UK) which was transferred from the Hong Kong and Shanghai Banking Corporation in 1988. In 1967, Midland bought a one-third share in Montague Trust, owner of the London merchant bank of Samuel Montague & Co, giving Midland a lead in broadening the spectrum of its banking services.

Midland entered the international travel business in 1971 when it joined with the Automobile Association and Trust House Forte in making a consortium bid for the denationalised travel agency Thomas Cook. In May 1972, Midland became owner of 70 per cent of Thomas Cook and its subsidiaries, and took over full ownership five years later.

Midland continued to develop its range of services and re-organise its branch network throughout the 1970s and 1980s. The corporate finance sector was re-organised in 1974 creating a team of specialists who could give greater support in handling the business of large corporate clients.

Faced with increased competition from foreign banks' representation in London, Midland opened representative offices in 14 financial centres throughout the world, and a new international division was created in 1974. Midland Financial Services was formed in Toronto Canada in 1975, and Associated Securities Finance in Australia was acquired in 1979. A majority share in Crocker National Corporation of California USA was acquired in 1981, but this investment proved a deep disappointment as the downturn in the local economy during the early 1980s hit Crocker's real estate loans hard, and Midland sold its interests to Wells Fargo in 1986.

When Midland reached its 150th anniversary in 1986, the banking environment was extremely challenging and competitive. Urgent changes were required to eradicate areas of weakness and to build on areas of strength. Overseas business generally suffered from the crisis in Third World debt repayments, heavy losses having been announced in 1983 and 1985, and the bank responded by making exceptional provisions against these debts of £1,016 million in 1987 and £846 million in the summer of 1989. Midland had now to increase its capital by raising more funds through a series of rights issues, totalling £1,075 million during the next two years. A 14.9 per cent interest in Midland was sold to the Hongkong and Shanghai Banking Corporation for £383 million.

At home, the pace of structural change accelerated to meet the needs of the market. Ninety new corporate banking centres were established between 1987 and 1991 each designed to focus on the requirements of medium sized business customers. In retail banking, branches were given a vital role in the active selling of the services of the group. In 1986 a 'new image' was introduced for branches, with a more spacious and attractive environment for customers. In March 1990, Midland Enterprise was launched to service the needs of small businesses, and by 1991 over 330 Enterprise centres had been established within the branch network.

N

NATIONAL FEDERATION OF INDEPENDENT FINANCIAL ADVISORS

This is the trade association of independent financial advisors.

NATIONAL SAVINGS BANK

The National Savings Bank operates through the Post Office and provides a range of savings and investment schemes such as:

- fixed interest savings certificates
- first option bonds
- childrens bonus bonds
- capital bonds
- income bonds
- pensioners guaranteed income bonds
- government stocks
- premium bonds

- investment accounts
- ordinary accounts
- index linked savings bonds
- index linked Government stock.

NATIONAL WESTMINSTER BANK

National Westminster Bank was officially born on New Year's Day 1970, when the new name and the now familiar three-arrowhead symbols appeared on 3,500 branches in the high streets of England and Wales, the Channel Islands and the Isle of Man, and the signboards of the District, National Provincial and Westminster Banks were taken down. The roots of the three banks, however, go back into the eighteenth and nineteenth centuries.

The District Bank

The District Bank was formed as the Manchester and Liverpool District Banking Company in 1829, and was the first joint-stock bank to be formed in England and Wales after the passing of the 1826 Act. The company was formed from the merger of three private banks, the District Union Banking Company, Christy Lloyd and Co and the Stockport and Cheshire Bank. The new bank, with a nominal capital of £3 million, opened on 1 December 1829. By the spring of 1830, the bank had opened new offices in Oldham, Liverpool and the potteries, and by the end of 1833 the Manchester Head Office stood at the centre of a network of 17 branches.

In 1834 the bank decided to dispense with issuing its own bank notes in favour of opening an account with the Bank of England. In spite of a difficult time as a result of some very substantial bad debts and the theft of £5,105 during 1834, the bank continued to prosper and embarked on a series of acquisition until by 1880, the year in which it adopted limited liability, the bank controlled 54 branches and sub-branches. It decided to move to premises in London in 1885, and a merger with the Leicester Banking Company took the number of branches to 118 by 1907.

The bank continued to prosper between the wars, and a second London office was opened in 1925. A merger with the County Bank in 1935 increased the paid up capital to almost £3 million and strengthened the bank's position so it could continue with its expansion of its branch operations throughout the Midlands, southern England and in Wales.

In 1962, the bank merged with the National Provincial Bank, and in 1970, became part of National Westminster Bank.

The National Provincial Bank

The National Provincial Bank was founded by a former Newcastle timber merchant by the name of Thomas Joplin in 1833. The bank's policy was to open branches throughout England and Wales, outside of the 65 mile limit around London specified by the legislation of 1826 and 1833. The first branch was opened in Gloucester in 1834, followed by Brecon and Walsall in the same year. By its second Annual General Meeting on 14 May 1835, the bank had 20 branches and sub-branches. Within three years, the National Provincial became the first truly national bank, with branches throughout England and Wales.

For the first 30 years the bank grew both by opening new branches and by a policy of absorbing local banking firms. During this period, more than 20 small banks were acquired, mostly in the west country and along the south coast. The bank decided to give up issuing its own bank notes in 1866.

The mergers continued throughout the next 50 years, until the merger with the Union of London and Smiths Bank brought the National Provincial to just under 700 branches and sub-branches. The most notable acquisition during the next 25 years was Coots & Co, acquired in 1920, and the Isle of Man Bank in 1961, but both of these continued to have their own Board of Directors and to operate independently of National Provincial.

The Westminster Bank

Early in 1833, William Robert Douglas, a member of a firm of Scottish merchants based in London, gathered a small committee of businessmen to consider the formation of a joint-stock bank in London. At the time it was far from certain that the terms of the Bank Charter Act, so hotly disputed between the Government and the Bank of England, were in the end to remove any possible obstacles to the establishment of joint-stock banks in London. By the final reading of the Bill on 26 August 1833, Douglas and his friends had already issued the prospectus of a bank to be designated the London and Westminster Bank, the first joint-stock bank to be formed in London.

From its foundation the bank experienced difficulties and hostility from the press, the private bankers and the Bank of England, and it was not until

1842 that the Bank of England agreed to open an account for the London and Westminster, and the joint-stock banks were not admitted to the London Clearing House until 1854.

Only six branches were opened between 1834 and 1836, and no further branches were opened until 1855, and only towards the end of the century did expansion of the network accelerate to reach 37 by the time of the amalgamation with London and County Bank in 1909. All the branches were within a 10 mile radius of London.

A series of amalgamations took place between 1909 and 1918 which produced a fully national bank with 700 branches throughout the country.

The history of the modern Westminster bank began in 1918, known until 1923 as the London and County Westminster Bank. It continued with a series of amalgamations and continued to open new branches as business and urban expansion demanded, and by 1939 there were approximately 1,100 branches.

After 1945 expansion in branches continued so that there were some 1,400 by the time of the merger with the National Provincial Bank in 1968. By 1956 every customer was receiving a machine-produced statement, and the bank was a leader in the change-over to computer accounting in the 1960s. It kept abreast of its rivals in the rapid widening of the financial services being offered to the public. In addition to its comprehensive British and Irish business, the Bank contributed to the National Westminster Bank its Foreign Bank with five branches in France and two in Belgium, all of which had been established over 60 years.

The relaxation of the moratorium on Bank mergers in the 1960s allowed the merger of the National Provincial and Westminster banks and the National Westminster Bank Ltd was registered on 19 March 1968. The branches of the District, National and Provincial and Westminster Banks were fully integrated, while Coutts, the Isle of Man Bank and the Ulster Bank continued to operate separately.

The branch network was rationalised to reduce the number from 3,600 at merger to 3,200 in 1979. Access cards made their appearance in 1972 and the computer linked 'service-till' network of cash machines was introduced in 1976.

National Westminster's most dramatic growth took place in international banking. Westminster's Foreign bank was renamed International Westminster Bank in 1973, adding to its French and Belgian branches offices in West Germany and Nassau. The bank was also represented in Australia, Bahrain, Canada, Greece, Hong Kong, Japan Mexico, Singapore, Spain,

USA and USSR. In 1975 it became the majority shareholder in Handelsband NW of Zurich and Global Bank AG of West Germany in 1977.

Related Banking Services Division contributed to the strong growth of the Bank in the 1970s with the acquisition of Lombard Banking, merged with the existing leasing and credit finance company to form Lombard North Central.

The 1980s were characterised by rapidly changing environments in the City of London and the financial market-places at home and abroad. Business Centres were established in 100 localities during 1986 and in 1989 the divisional structure was reorganised into three business sectors — UK Financial Services, International Business and Corporate and Institutional Banking, to focus the bank's operations on the distinctive needs of both private and commercial customers.

New and enlarged services appearing during the 1980s included Home Loans (1980) Piggy, On line and Investment accounts (1983) Special Reserve accounts, free banking in credit and selective Saturday opening (1985). With deregulation of financial markets in 1986 the Bank introduced share dealing computer terminals for customers and under the Financial Services Act chose, in 1988 to become an independent intermediary, necessitating the sale of its unit trust subsidiary. The changes wrought in the city during the 1980s prompted the bank to acquire stock-broking and jobbing firms and to include its County Bank services within NatWest Investment Bank incorporated in 1986.

OFFICIAL RECEIVER

The official receiver is an officer of the Department of Trade who oversees the winding-up of insolvent businesses. The official receiver may act as liquidator or appoint another person to undertake this role.

ONE-STOP SHOPS

These are intended to bring together a national network of local centres that will offer a full range of business support services available through local agencies such as the TEC, local enterprise agency and Chamber of Commerce. Their aim will be to help all businesses including those who wish to develop and grow. A pilot programme of six centres was opened in 1993, and it is intended to extend this to 23.

OVERDRAFT

An overdraft is a means by which additional funding is made available through an individual's or a business's current (cheque) account. Overdrafts are useful for short-term cash flow difficulties, but can be expensive. An overdraft is usually agreed for a limited period of time, and extended only at the bank's discretion. Overdrafts can be 'called in' at any time if the bank believes that the business or the individual is no longer able to clear the amount outstanding, or if it is no longer in the individual's interests for the overdraft to continue.

OVERHEADS

This term is used to describe a business's fixed costs, that is costs which are incurred irrespective of how much the business manufactures or sells. Such costs would include rent on premises, heat and light, administrative costs and in some circumstances, wages.

P

PARTNERSHIP

A partnership is the relationship between two or more people who are in business jointly with a view to profit. Each partner is 'jointly and severally liable' for the debts of the business, and that means that a creditor may pursue any or all of the partners for the debts. While it is not a requirement to have a partnership agreement, it is usually considered foolish to engage in this type of business without first entering into a partnership deed. This will lay out clearly the rights and responsibilities of each partner, and will provide the basis on which problems can be solved should the relationship between the partners break down at any time. It will also help to prevent arguments. The Partnership Act provides a framework that can be used to design a partnership deed, but partners are free to make any sort of agreement they like — the Act will only step in if the partnership agreement is silent or ambiguous on a point in dispute.

PROFESSIONAL INDEMNITY INSURANCE

This type of insurance is taken out by people such as doctors, solicitors and accountants to provide protection against negligence of themselves or their employees for which a client may sue them.

PROFIT

For the majority of trading organisations, the maximisation of profit is the primary motivating factor. Without profit, a business will quickly become insolvent, and the owners of the business or a sole trader or a partnership will become bankrupt. However, the concept of profit is not one that is always understood, and is often confused with having money in the bank, but cash and profit are two different things.

In order for a business to make a profit, it must be able to receive sufficient revenue from its sales to cover both the purchase and manufacturing costs of its goods, plus all its fixed costs, (or overheads), such as rent, heat and light, advertising, administrative costs, and its wages. Some of these cost can be difficult to predict, and owners of small businesses often overestimate the amount of profit that they could make.

It is necessary for all businesses to keep track of their profits as the year progresses, or they may get a nasty shock at the end of year. This is particularly true of a sole trader who must be able to take money out of the business during the course of the year to pay his personal expenses and have money on which to live.

In order to keep track of the profits made during the year, the business will need to make good use of a record-keeping system and to extract an interim profit and loss statement on a regular basis in order to monitor the performance of the business.

PUBLIC LIABILITY INSURANCE

Public liability insurance indemnifies a business against claims made by visitors or members of the public who are killed or injured, or who have their property damaged while on the business premises.

R

READY MADE COMPANIES

It is possible to avoid some of the delays and hassle of setting up a company from scratch by buying a ready made company that has never traded.

REGISTERED OFFICE

The registered office is the address that has been declared to the Registrar of Companies as being the registered office of a company. This address should appear on all company stationery and should be displayed at the office premises.

REGISTRAR OF COMPANIES

The registrar of companies keeps all the records of companies registered in England and Wales at Companies House. It will allocate a registration number and incorporation certificate, and keep the records of the end of year accounts.

S

THE SMALL BUSINESS BUREAU

This is a pressure group affiliated to the Conservative Party. It produces a bi-monthly newspaper and provides an advisory service to members.

THE STOCK EXCHANGE

The London Stock Exchange plays a big part in maintaining London's role as the leading international financial centre, with roots which stretch back to the sixteenth century when the first joint-stock company was formed. Since that time, the Exchange has brought together those wanting to raise finance (whether industry or Government) with those who wish to invest.

The Exchange was originally constituted by a Deed of Settlement in 1802 and carried on business for the benefit of its proprietors, the individual members of the Stock Exchange. However, the Exchange became a private limited company in November 1986, prompting the change from being a 'member association' to becoming a non-profit making company. Member firms became shareholders of the Exchange, with each firm holding a single vote. The Exchange generates its own income through a variety of sources including listing and membership fees, revenue from its settlement operations and from the sale of information services. Its customers for these products span the whole of the investment world, from major financial institutions to private investors.

In 1991, the original Deed of Settlement was replaced by a Memorandum and Articles of Association. This led to the replacement of the governing Council of the Exchange with a modern Board of Directors, which is drawn both from the Exchange's executive and from its customer and user base. This ensures that all the major categories of the Exchange's customers can contribute to the decisions which affect the way the Exchange operates.

In addition to providing a market-place where listed securities can be traded efficiently, the exchange provides the infrastructure to make the market work. That includes maintaining market rules and regulations, providing services for market users, together with a secure and timely means of settling share transactions.

The Exchange provides a market for the buying and selling of more than 7,000 securities, with the main markets in UK and international equities. Operating in the European time zone, the Exchange holds a vital position in the world of international finance between New York and Tokyo. More overseas companies are listed in London than on any other stock exchange and around 65 per cent of all shares traded outside their home country is done via London. The figure rises to more than 90 per cent within Europe.

In October 1986 the major reforms known as 'Big Bang' revolutionised securities trading in London. The traditional methods of the stock market, with business conducted face to face on a market floor, were replaced by new technology that allowed the market's participants to trade from their own dealing rooms. Along with these changes, major overseas securities firms and UK and overseas banks became increasingly involved in the equities markets. Many bought member firms, allowing them to compete with overseas brokers from a larger capital base. In addition to this, the Financial Services Act of 1986 transformed the regulation of the market-place and gave the Exchange clearly defined powers and responsibilities.

Each year, UK and overseas companies turn to London to raise capital for their business or to have their shares more widely marketed and traded. Companies raise money through the issue of shares on the Exchange's primary market, as we discussed in Chapter 4. The Exchange also lists eurobonds. These are issued by way of selective marketing to chosen financial institutions and underwritten by an international syndicate of banks. In addition to being sold in their country of origin, they are also offered on a significant scale in other countries. Eurobonds are normally listed to ensure that securities are available to the widest possible range of investors. A number of institutional investors also have a policy of buying only listed bonds. Some 2,400 eurobonds are listed in London.

Four basic types of securities are listed and traded on the Exchange:

- UK or domestic equities — ordinary shares issued by UK companies
- overseas equities — ordinary shares issued by non-UK companies
- UK gilts — securities issued by the UK Government to raise money to fund any shortfall in public expenditure
- bonds of fixed interest stocks — usually by companies or local authorities. They entitle the owner to regular interest payments and the repayment of a fixed sum at a given date in the future.

Once a UK company has been admitted to the Official List, its ordinary shares are traded on the domestic equity market which is operated and regulated by the Exchange. Around 30,000 transactions take place in the market each day. In 1992, the average daily turnover in UK and Irish equities stood at £1.7 billion.

Trading of UK equities is mainly based on the system of competing 'market makers'. Throughout the trading day, market makers are obliged to make continuous firm buying and selling prices in the securities in which they are registered. They deal with brokers (also members of the Exchange) who act on behalf of clients, or directly with institutional investors. Market makers make their income from the difference between the buying and selling prices they offer.

The market makers' buying and selling prices are displayed on the Exchange's automated price information system, SEAQ (Stock Exchange Automated Quotations) This system displays continuously updated price quotations in UK securities and reports on shares traded, with the best prices offered and bid for each stock highlighted automatically. Brokers can deal at these prices over the telephone.

TOPIC, the Exchange's screen based information service, and other distributors of information present SEAQ and other market information to users. For the trading of listed UK equities in which turnover has proved to be insufficient to support the market making system, the Exchange introduced the Stock Exchange Alternative Trading Service (SEATS) in November 1992. Distributed via TOPIC, the service shows current orders, company information, the past trading activity for each stock, the name of the sole market maker and the two-way prices quoted for each security.

London is the largest market in the world for trading non-domestic equities. Some 500 securities are eligible for trading on SEAQ International, the Exchange's international market. Every day there are a total of 8,500 non-domestic equity transactions in London, with an average daily turnover of £1.3 billion. More than 50 market makers from major international securities houses quote instantly updated process on SEAQ international which is also displayed on TOPIC and by other distributors of information worldwide.

Share prices are usually quoted in the home currency of each country sector, and transactions are settled through the local settlement system. The average bargain size on SEAQ International reflects the fact that much of the business carried out is from major financial institutions. In 1992 the average size of bargain was over £150,000, compared with £50,000 for UK equities on SEAQ.

As with UK equities, the gilt-edged market is conducted on-screen, with trading carried out by telephone. A network of gilt-edged market makers (GEMMS), recognised by the Bank of England, makes a continuous market in government securities. The prices are displayed by a computer system independent of SEAQ, but still administered by the Exchange. Activity in the gilts market has increased considerably in recent years with average daily turnover reaching over £5 billion in 1992.

In the market for fixed interest securities, market makers register with the Exchange. They have to offer to buy and sell a fixed quantity of stock at a firm price to other member firms, but are not obliged to buy from or sell to other market makers. In 1992 the market had an average daily turnover of £340 million.

History shows that the Exchange has grown with the City, reflecting and promoting the development of the financial markets. It is no longer the gentlemen's club of old, but a modern commercial organisation at the forefront of world finance.

T

TAX

A philosopher once wrote that there are only two certainties in life, death and taxes. Taxation is the means by which a government raises the finance it needs to undertake its public spending programme for such things as the health service, the armed forces, social security payments, etc. Broadly speaking, taxes can be divided into two main areas, direct and indirect taxation. Direct taxation is levied on the income of individuals and the self-employed, and corporation tax on company profits. Indirect taxation is levied on goods and comes in the form of VAT (see below) and excise duty on such things as cigarettes, tobacco and alcohol. In addition, local authorities are empowered to raise taxation at a local level to fund the spending programmes on such things as education, emergency services and highways. Local authorities raise funds largely through the Council Tax, levied on domestic premises, and Unified Business Rates, which are levied on commercial and businesses premises.

TAX RETURNS

Tax is calculated by means of an annual tax return which is completed by an individual or company detailing income or profits for the year and any allowable expenses that may be deducted.

THEFT INSURANCE

This type of insurance provides cover against loss or damage to the contents of business premises as a result of theft. The insurance company will usually require proof of forced entry or exit from the premises.

TRADE AND INDUSTRY, DEPARTMENT OF

This is the government department which is responsible for industry throughout the country. It provides help and advice in many areas through a series of regional offices which can be found in the Yellow Pages.

U

UNIT TRUSTS

Unit trusts are a means of investing in the stock market which allows the individual investor to spread the risk by investing in a fund created and managed by an investment management group. Instead of buying shares directly, the investor can put the money into a fund which is then invested in the stock market. The risk is spread because the fund is invested in a much wider selection of shares than an individual could normally achieve on their own. Dividends and capital gains made by the fund are then distributed to investors either on a monthly, quarterly or annual basis, depending on the rules of the individual fund.

V

VALUE ADDED TAX (VAT)

VAT is a form of indirect taxation which was introduced to replace purchase tax when the UK joined the European Community. VAT is levied at each stage of production and distribution and reflects the value that is added to the goods at each stage. There are currently four levels of value added tax: full rate (17.5 per cent), fuel tax (8 per cent), zero rated and tax exempt.

VENTURE CAPITAL

Sometimes described as risk capital, venture capital is additional funding sought by a business for expansion of the business or for development of a particular process or product. Unlike a loan which is repayable over a set time, venture capital is usually exchanged for a share in the business equity or a cut of the profits from the business.

VOLUNTARY ARRANGEMENTS

If a business finds that it is unable to pay its debts, it is possible to enter into a voluntary agreement with the creditors to pay a percentage of the debts in full settlement. This has to be arranged through an authorised insolvency practitioner, and once agreed, is legally binding. It is useful to prevent bankruptcy or compulsory winding up of the business.

W

WORKERS CO-OPERATIVES

These are formed when the employees of a company take over the running of a business, often when a section of a company is threatened with closure. They are similar in form to a management buy-out, but in this case, all the employees become shareholders of the company, and usually devise some co-operative form of management.

Index